WROTE THE BOOK, MOVIE, RAISED, NOW THE BLOG...

21st Century musings
from an exhausted Renaissance Woman

Shamim Sarif

enlightenment press

To follow Shamim's current blogs, please go to:

www.shamimsarif.com

or

http://www.facebook.com/pages/Shamim-Sarif/67470360408?ref=ts

For Hanan, Ethan and Luca. In gratitude for an amazing journey; sometimes hard, mostly fun, but always together.

CONTENTS

Introduction

Why bother putting together a collection of blogs that you can read on the internet? Well, I am still touched by all the people who took the time to let me know my blogs made them snort coffee through their noses, or made them get arrested for laughing maniacally in internet cafes. And I've lost count of the number of readers who asked me to put together a book of these blogs (Ok, it was three of you) so it could be enjoyed on a train, in bed, or any of those places where an old-fashioned book just works better.

My wife Hanan and I made two feature films in just over two years – 'I Can't Think Straight' and 'The World Unseen'. We have our own production company, Enlightenment Productions, and are very much independent producers. When the films were released, we didn't have huge advertising or hundreds of cinema screens – but the films had an overwhelmingly positive response from audiences, and we began to experience a trickle, then a deluge of emails (I may exaggerate just slightly, but only just) from fans of the movies.

On the advice of someone more technologically and socially savvy than me, I set up a Facebook Fan page, and in the spring of 2009, I started writing a blog and posting it on that page and my website. Prior to email, I used to write to my friends using a fountain pen and airmail paper. I am not eighty years old, but I always had a certain attachment to what I saw as a more civilized world, the gentle rustle of paper pulled from an envelope, the romantic sweep of ink in cursive script…you get the idea. The advent of email and children put an end to any further messing about with pen and ink.

But it did take me a while to reconcile myself to the idea of blogging, and my early attempts were short, and held a tinge of slight embarrassment that I was chatting to people I didn't know. I got over that after several weeks of rehab in an intensive, self-help, 12-step social networking clinic and I have included just a few of those first blogs here, so the blog year starts in earnest at the end of March.

By the end of the year, in fact, I did get to know a lot of the fans – from the interactions from the blogs, and also from the sheer dedication, hard work, and support offered to us and the films by so many people who were touched by the movies. I thank them for their support, and I thank Hanan for making every one of these adventures possible.

A Note From Lisa Ray

Working with Shamim and Hanan has left me with the sensation of discovering a new home: a sanctuary bordered by security and love, with a centre of creative zaniness. Better than home. I didn't have to take out the garbage.

Hanan was in charge of rubbish removal. Like any great producer, she shielded the creative team from the latest on-set crisis. Leaving Shamim free to gently guide Sheetal and I through two diverse scripts.

Shamim has all the qualities to be a splendid director - or a pirate. I joke but the two careers overlap. Shamim led me into new territory. We navigated calm and turbulent conditions. We weren't sure what bounty awaited us, but like any accomplished captain, Shamim never lost her focus. Or humour.

So while directing two films is not the same as leading a crew of privateers, there is a common requirement for both missions: discreet audacity. Otherwise known as courage. And insight.

And to think it may never have happened.

I was studying drama in London. My agent, Aude, called me, excited about a script. It was called 'The World Unseen' and I had an appointment to meet the producer in Chelsea the next day.

So I showed up.

Hanan, all dynamic energy and curls, greeted me warmly. I sat down.

'So what did you think of the script?'

'I didn't read it.'

Curls shivered indignantly.

'Well, then what are you doing here?'

'I have an appointment to meet you.'

'Why?'

I remember I am a student of drama and practise my 'inscrutable' rather than 'disoriented' look.

'My agent told me it's a great script' I try. 'Um, I'm Lisa, Lisa Ray' I add, lamely.
My name is currency in some parts of the world. But in this tony Chelsea Chinese restaurant, Hanan just looks at me like I served her soggy spring rolls.

'But you haven't read it'

Sigh. 'No. But my agent said you wanted to meet me.'

'But you haven't read it'

You can imagine the rest of the conversation.

It was a Mexican stand-off between an Indian-Pole and Palestinian. Destined to end badly.

Except...

I returned to my flat, indignant. And intrigued. I picked up 'The World Unseen' and began to read. And I didn't stop until I had finished the book in a single seating. Then I read the script. And I understood.

I understood Hanan's passion and single-mindedness.

It's these qualities in both Shamim and Hanan that has moved me. And motivated me. I am proud to have worked with both these extraordinary women. I am grateful to have them in my life.

Cast of Characters

For those of you who come to this book fresh, and haven't got a clue who I am or why you should be reading this – thank you for taking the time, and here's a quick run down of the real-life characters who pop up in the book:

Hanan – my wife, my muse, my inspiration, and chief motivator. Basically, she makes the characters in an Ayn Rand novel look like chronic under-achievers.

Lisa Ray – lead actress in both films I wrote and directed – The World Unseen and I Can't Think Straight. Friend, creative co-conspirator and dispenser of nuggets of existentialist wisdom.

Sheetal Sheth – also a lead actress in both films. Target of Hanan's bewilderment and newly-minted icon to thousands of lesbians worldwide, especially in China.

Leonie Casanova – singer/songwriter who contributed songs to both movies. A close friend, and close emotional relative of her namesake, the lion.

Aida Kattan – Hanan's youngest sister, champion of our movies, head of marketing and festivals, friend to a myriad of fans, and Enlightenment Employee of the Month every month, despite receiving only To Do lists and no pay.

Ethan and Luca – our sons. Bringers of joy, love and rubber spiders to the Sarif-Kattan household.

READY TO READ?

January 19th

PEOPLE OFTEN ASK ME what I like to read. I should say that what I like to read and what I usually end up reading are two different things. Has anyone tried reading the notes from the Film Council on filling in an application? That's an hour of your life you'll never get back. And then the children usually come home bearing reams of paper, advising us that there's a football match tomorrow ('Mummy, I need shin pads?' 'Not if you run away from the ball') or that there's a play this week ('Mummy I need a 1960's top', 'I don't think people wore tops in the 60s sweetheart') or that someone in school has hair crawling with lice. It's all a far cry from the romance and sweeping drama of literature. By the end of the day I usually collapse into bed and enjoy just looking at the cover of the book I am intending to read (currently Ronald Harwood on screenplay adaptations). As for online reading...well, I have no time, it would have to be brilliantly written, and laugh-out-loud funny would help too. One daily blog makes the cut. www. peachesandcoconuts.com I declare an interest. Deborah Goldstein is an old (but incredibly well-preserved) friend of mine and Hanan's. The woman can write. Check it out and let me know what you think. When you've finished this...

Deborah and Shamim admire each other's blogs much more after a bottle of red wine.

AND THE AWARD GOES TO…

February 8th

SAFTA night in Pretoria, South Africa, and my first challenge was getting in and out of a car while wearing a long black dress and (sort of) heels while being broadcast on live television. Are there schools for this? Or an evening course?! The nominees were taken to an underground car park, hustled into a series of Mercedes and then driven around to the front of the theatre where - wait for it - people screamed as Hanan and I got out of the car onto the red carpet. I was more than a touch disconcerted. Had they noticed a ladder in my tights? Did my make-up free face scare them?! No, they screamed for everyone, it turned out. We were accosted by an excitable TV interviewer.

'Don't worry,' Hanan had told me in the car. 'Just talk about the film.' I had this in mind when her first, helium-stoked question came.

'Who designed that divine dress?' I had no idea. I only know I've worn it to the last 5 black tie things I've had to go to…I thought things could only improve with the next question and smiled bravely.

'Ladies, you look so stunning, where are your men?' Oh dear.

But it was a great night, and I was so happy Hanan was there. We swept the awards, winning eleven. We were only nominated for ten. You have to love this place. David Dennis (Jacob), Grethe Fox (Madeleine) and Natalie Becker (Farah) were there from the cast, and I was so happy that production design, costume design and cinematography won too. Very well deserved. We staggered home (heels in hands) around 1am. A memorable way to celebrate our 13th anniversary.

Danielle (Costume), Tanya (Production Design) David (Best Supporting Actor), Grethe (Best Ensemble), Hanan (Producer) and Natalie (Best Supporting Actress) all know where their clothes came from…

THE SUN ALWAYS SHINES ON TV (AT LEAST IN CAPE TOWN)

February 10th

DAY TWO IN SUNNY Cape Town, and a round of interviews. Now that we have won 11 SAFTA awards (yes, after 10 nominations - not everyone can manage it) lots of TV stations here want to interview me. I know in my head this is good for the movie, but I can't help feeling I have a better face for radio. However, I gamely hold in my stomach and try and sound intelligent while trying not to direct the cameraman. Then off to another radio interview with Natalie Becker (Farah in the movie). This all gets a bit out of control, but in a good way, as Natalie is on good form, and she then jumps onto her pink moped (see photo below, I really don't make this stuff up) to join me at the Cape Town premiere.

After all that hard work (!) it was time for a celebratory drink with our World Unseen team including Natalie and Shaz Van Zanten, the ex-Miss Southern Africa who was our housemate in Cape Town and apart from being our own statuesque, blonde playboy bunny, also looked after us and the boys so amazingly well. Back in Johannesburg tonight, and off to bed as I am up in 4 hours to go on breakfast TV. If the sight of me on 4 hours sleep doesn't encourage people to wake up to their radios instead, I don't know what will...

Natalie Becker ('Farah') models the new 'World Unseen Barbie' moped.

UPCOMING SCREENINGS

March 13th

So IN THE WHIRLWIND of work and children and life, special screenings rise up out of my calendar like oases in the desert, mostly because it's a break from our normal routine, except that we don't actually have a normal routine...Next Saturday 21st March, I should be on a train to Manchester for a charity screening of 'The World Unseen' arranged by the irrepressible Rod Priestley (Sergeant Stewart in the movie) in association with our very own fledgling Sarif-Kattan Foundation. Rod was, of course, robbed of his Best Supporting Actor Oscar this year but has been incredibly gracious about that. That trip involves a train journey in the company of

1) Hanan (so I should take my laptop and work like mad)

2) Exec Producer and dear friend Katherine (so I should take the laptop but catch up with her)

3) My sister Anouchka (so I should forget work, kick back and complain about our parents)

4) her new boyfriend (so I should definitely close the laptop and scrutinise him to make sure he's good enough) and

5) Leonie Casanova (so I should ditch all the above and just beg her to sing to us the entire way there).

Anyway, you get the gist. It'll be fun, and it will, I am sure, be inspirational thanks to the amazing charity it supports (http://www.justgiving.com/thebuckers).

Rod Priestley prepares to interrogate Shamim's sister's boyfriend.

BLACK TIE & JEANS

March 19th

TIRED OF GOING TO the movies in jeans? Bored with wiping salt from your popcorn on your old T-shirt? No, me neither. However, I am going to have to dress up for the 5th of May. What is it, you ask? The award for the lesbian who eats the most and blogs the least? My mother's 30th birthday (again!)? No, better than that, it is a charity screening of a wonderful movie called 'The World Unseen', in aid of the Nelson Mandela Children's Fund. At BAFTA in Piccadilly, London and brought to you by the Sarif-Kattan Foundation. And if I have to swap my jeans and shirt for 'black tie' attire (can I possibly recycle the SAFTA dress one more time?!) then I think some of you should join me. Tickets are £50, but all for a great cause, and you get a wonderful movie (did I already mention that?), Q&A, book signing, performance from the stunningly talented Leonie Casanova, raffles, drinks, canapes and goody bags. So if you are in London, and you can make it, come and join us there. Tickets from info@enlightenment-productions.com. I would write more but I have a cold and am sniffling over my keyboard with just a bit of self-pity, hoping my producer will suggest that I call it a night and get to bed. Or, even better, offer to rub Vicks on my chest.... Ok, neither of those is happening. I am sneaking out of the room against the wall before she notices I am gone.

Suitable attire for the BAFTA screening…

NOW I KNOW HOW BEYONCE FEELS (OKAY, MAYBE NOT BEYONCE, EXACTLY)

March 30th

FRIDAY NIGHT WAS OFFICIALLY our BSE, and that has nothing to do with mad cows or any other disease, it stands for Best Screening Ever. To those of you who were in the audience at the BFI, thank you for screaming and clapping as I came out to introduce the film. Of course, the fact that my truly rock star-like wife was behind me may have induced the applause, or maybe it was Nina Wadia of Eastenders fame, who was behind her, who caused the screaming. But I like to think it was me. And please don't write in to tell me otherwise, OK?!

Seriously, though, there was a lot of good will in that packed cinema, and the audience (obviously 450 people of incredibly good taste, not to mention a keen sense of irony) laughed from the time the credits rolled to the time the movie ended. And in the right places. It was tremendous to feel such a strong interaction from the audience and it's moments like that that really do make it all worthwhile.

We did a Q&A and then a book signing, and then had a drinks reception. By the time the first sip of white wine hit my stomach, I hadn't eaten in 9 hours (for someone who spends each meal planning the next, that's scary) because the earlier part of the day had been spent doing radio and press interviews. I resisted the urge to whine and pass out, and ended up meeting some wonderful people and finally got home very late to collapse. Our house looked as if it had been raided by Sudanese rebels, which gave us a clue that our children had not behaved at their best while we were out...but we were still on a high, though as I lay there on the bed, telling Hanan that I was too excited to even close my eyes, I am embarrassed to say I fell asleep before I finished the sentence...I bet real rock stars can stay awake past 11pm, right?

In her first viewing of I Can't Think Straight, Nina Wadia realises that the movie is not just about a spitting housekeeper...

TAMING THE LION

March 31st

A LOT OF YOU HAVE HEARD me talking about the brilliant singer-songwriter Leonie Casanova, but you may wonder how we actually met her, and how it happened that she inspired us to set up Enlightenment Records. If you are not wondering about this, then stop reading now and go and watch her music videos on this page. If you're not wondering after that, we'll call it a day. Everyone else can read my new screenplay below of how we met the Lioness as she is known to those who truly know her…

FADE IN. THREE YEARS EARLIER. NIGHT.

Hanan and Shamim are at home. Hanan is working on her computer, while Shamim is whining about being tired. The phone RINGS for the 4th time in 10 minutes. Shamim picks up.

SHAMIM: Alma, we are not coming out with you tonight. I'm tired.

ALMA: You can't miss this. It's a group of famous film people and one of the actor's girlfriend is singing.

SHAMIM: It's 9.30. Who goes out at 9.30?

ALMA: Everyone except my grandmother. Are you 80?

Stung by this, and faced with 2 more hours of work, Shamim caves in and goes to Notting Hill with Hanan.

INTERIOR. COOL CLUB. NIGHT.

In the dim lighting, Shamim ends up sitting with a couple of actors and weeping from self-pitying exhaustion into her £20 drink. The MC introduces the singer.

SHAMIM: Leonie Casanova? What kind of name is that?

The singer walks on stage. She looks like a goddess. Casanova is clearly her real name. She opens her mouth to sing. Shamim stops weeping and stares, amazed by the beautiful song that is being woven out over the audience. When the set is finished, Shamim is humbled and vows never to whine again (a promise she will break within 24 hours). Leonie walks off stage, to be accosted by Hanan.

HANAN: Hi Leonie. You were amazing. We are making a film called 'The World Unseen' and we'd like you to write a song for it.

LEONIE: When are you shooting?

SHAMIM (to herself): No idea.

HANAN: Soon.

LEONIE: What's the budget?

SHAMIM (to herself): No idea.

HANAN: Small.

LEONIE: I'd love to, I just need to pop to the ladies room.

HANAN: Not till you sign here.

And the rest is history. Seriously, Leonie has a rare combination of accessible melodies and poetic lyrics that could make Leonard Cohen weep. And her single 'Broken' (remixed from 'The World Unseen') is now on Itunes. Check it out, and spread the word.

Leonie Casanova during the shoot of her music video 'Broken' walking across a screen showing her own character in 'The World Unseen'. (What a brilliant idea from the genius director of this video).

SWISS CLIMBING

April 17th

I HAD A SWISS DAY. No, not running through the alps with a cuckoo clock, but visiting the Aqua Park with our children. Forget the alps, the lake, the fresh air. You haven't lived till you've been enclosed in 8,000 square feet of plastic with 1000 Swiss teenagers, climbing 300 stairs at a time while carrying an inflatable boat the size of Texas. That little sojourn took around 4 hours, during which my worst Howard Hughes-type phobias about personal hygiene, re-used water, and overheated, bacteria-filled atmospheres were confirmed...I tried to focus on the excitement on my boys' faces, until the little one's crumpled in fear as we prepared to descend the black water slide. I had just walked up 789 stairs carrying a boat that could have been a relic from the Titanic, and I was not about to walk back down so I convinced him it was a safe and fun ride down. As my karmic punishment for lying to my own child, I was invited to dinner at our Swiss neighbour's house, which was not that bad except that I am anti-social at the best of times, and especially around people who only speak French, unless they look like Emmanuelle Beart. We ate raclette, which is melted Swiss cheese, very delicious and enough to fuel a hike up a Swiss mountain, or indeed a water slide. Luckily, my wife is fluent in French, so I was able to sit and watch her admiringly...

Hanan, speaker of 5 languages, prevents me from escaping from the Swiss neighbours…

STUFFED

April 21st

So OUR FIRST DAY BACK in the office, and I started playing this game with Hanan that she is entirely unconscious of, in which I try to deal with her emails faster than she sends me new ones. It's like running in quicksand. Just as I was surfacing for air, my parents and sister called from the Italian place downstairs. The highlight of that lunch (other than the pasta) was that my sister Anouchka told them about her new boyfriend. Just the word 'boyfriend' was a relief to my mother after my atrocious news of 13 years ago, until my sister pretended he was black, and my mother protested that that was like 'the Hanan situation.'

'Is Hanan black?' I asked my dad, but he was busy asking if Anouchka would consider eloping (the cost of weddings runs high, I guess). Back to work, while fielding calls from the kids:

'Can I watch TV?'

'Have you done your homework?'

'Sort of'

'What does that mean?'

'Kind of'

'No TV.'

And then off to an early dinner with Hanan's father and the kids. It is illegal to be from any Arab country and not order enough food for a wedding banquet. I wished my sister and the boyfriend would show up as we could have thrown the reception right there. Anyway, it would have been rude not to eat it, right? So now I am typing furiously to work off those extra calories. My fingers definitely look thinner...

A different meal on 'The World Unseen' set. From left, clockwise: Nandana Sen, Sheetal Sheth, Natalie Becker, Lisa Ray, me, Brigid (co-producer), Hanan, and Leonie Casanova. My sister's boyfriend in in the back ;)

LEONIE CASANOVA SHAKES IT

April 26th

So KELLY MOSS, co-writer of the movie 'I Can't Think Straight', sent me the link to Beyonce's 'Single Ladies' video about 3 months ago. My first thought was, haven't music videos come a long way since Abba? That's not really true, since before going into directing Leonie Casanova's videos of 'Broken' and 'Little Feeling', I spent time on You Tube trying to educate myself about how music videos have evolved since Karen Carpenter. Quite a bit, was the answer to that. Anyway, I digress, as usual. Back to the story, and we're in the car the other day with Leonie, going to a meeting with music executive people, and Leonie tells me how Single Ladies was filmed in one continuous shot.

'So who's this Beyonce?' Hanan asked. Leonie looked pained, as she realised that she'd just signed to Enlightenment Records, a company run by someone whose last album purchase was quite possibly Barry White. In the meantime, I was considering how fit you have to be to shake all that booty for 4 minutes continuously. I may have run a red light while thinking about it, but it didn't matter because a light of a different kind had gone on above Hanan's head.

'I know Beyonce!' she exclaimed. 'She's that new Russian singer, right?'

Thank God the child locks were working, because Leonie tried to throw herself out of the car, and it was moving pretty fast...Anyway, you can see Leonie shaking her own booty at the end of the 'Little Feeling' video posted on this very page and then you can see her lying seductively on a pool table in 'Broken'. We may not have had quite the same budget as that Russian girl, but we've come a long way from Abba, baby...

Leonie Casanova clarifies in which direction Shamim would like her to shake her assets.

THE WORLD UNSEEN OF A WRITER

May 1st

Dorothy PARKER ONCE SAID that if you have a friend who is an aspiring writer, the second-biggest favour you can do them is to give them a copy of 'The Elements of Style'. The first-biggest favour is to shoot them now, while they're happy...This crossed my mind the other morning as I sat at home, in front of my laptop screen. Banished from the office to finish the screenplay of The Dreaming Spires, I was descending into a mist of despair as I realised I had forgotton how to put one word in front of the other. And it was only 9.30 am. I put on some music, trying to evoke the mood of lost love and mortal rejection being felt by my character at that moment. Now I was just missing Hanan. To take my mind off the vast distance between myself and my true love (about one mile, but that's not the point) I stared at my keyboard and realised it could probably use a clean. Did I dare abandon the moment of writerly struggle and go for the cleaning fluid and cotton buds? I rose from my chair...the phone rang. Hanan.

'How many pages have you done?' she asked chirpily.

'I don't know how to write any more!' I wailed.

'Just focus,' she said. 'Take your time. You have till lunch'

I put the phone down with renewed resolve. Tapped a few lines. Deleted them. Then watched emails floating in. There was one from a man in Nigeria offering to split $170 million dollars with me if I would just give him my bank account details. I considered whether I might get my cheque book out. I rose from my chair... the phone rang.

'How many pages?' Hanan wanted to know. I shifted uneasily, scanning the corners of the room. She has a webcam watching me, I swear.

'It's not like writing emails to Nigerians, you know," I replied, stung. 'It's hard.'

She said nothing but sniffed, a sniff that held in it all the meaning of 'Hard? Hard is waking up with no work, no food, no prospects and you are sitting in a lovely flat in peace and quiet doing what you always said you wanted to do...'

'But it's going fine,' I offered, into the silence. And you know what? After that, it did...

Standing with my wife on one side and a big Styrofoam copy of 'The World Unseen' in German makes it all worthwhile...

FREEDOM IS A STATE OF MIND

May 6th

REALLY, THE THEME OF 'The World Unseen' is freedom, breaking conventions, the emancipation of women. This occurred to me as I lay writhing on the bed last night, hauling on a pair of control-top tights that wouldn't come up past my thighs. Hanan walked in while I was in this compromised position and I stared at her (I was too exhausted by the exertion to actually speak) hoping she would emancipate me.

'We have to leave in five minutes,' she said.

I heaved myself up and into a long black sheath of an evening dress, noticing that my internal organs were screaming for oxygen. Breathing could wait. I had a BAFTA black tie charity screening of 'The World Unseen' to get to.

When we actually got there, there were paparazzi hanging around outside. As I stood with Hanan and the team, blinded by popping flashbulbs and photographers fighting for eyelines, I wondered briefly what on earth they were doing. Had my dress and pointy shoes and slick of lipstick (found in the back of the medicine cabinet, in a shade that was cool in 1997) actually turned me into Angelina Jolie? Or were they all on drugs? Or waiting for somebody else? I had no time to ponder this as we had drinks and canapes to get to, interviews and book-signings to do and finally, a movie to watch. We took our eldest son along, since he has quite a role in the movie, as Miriam's son, and it was the first time he'd seen himself on a big screen. He fidgeted during the talking scenes, watched open-mouthed during the police scenes and covered his eyes with a loud 'Eugh, gross!' that echoed through the cinema when Miriam and Amina kissed. Since this screening was in aid of a children's charity (the Nelson Mandela Children's Fund) I didn't think it was appropriate to put duct tape on his mouth, so I tried giving him the look of steel that my mother used to subdue me with, but he only rolled his eyes. Luckily, Leonie Casanova was about to perform, and after listening to 'Broken' sung live over the end credits, we were all a lot happier. As we clapped and cheered, I noticed that Leonie was singing in her stockinged feet, stilettos abandoned by her seat. I guess there was some female emancipation after all...

Hanan (producer), Lisa Tchenguiz (exec producer), Daisy Allsop (associate producer), Leonie Casanova, Katherine Priestley (exec producer) and Shamim Sarif (enslaved, stockinged, stiletto-heeled writer/director) outside BAFTA…

BULLET POINT BLOG

May 9th

S<small>O</small> AS I STAGGERED in from the park with two children, two scooters, two remote controlled cars and the knowledge that there were two squashed bananas waiting to be scraped off the bottom of my rucksack, Hanan asked me if I'd written a blog today. I resisted the urge to say, yes, I dictated it into my remote controlled Macbook as I chased after runaway kids, and that it was all swear words. Instead, I asked my wife what I should write a blog about. She looked at me, and I could feel the wheels in her mind whirring..I waited, hopeful she would suggest something exciting, funny, brilliant. Here was her list:

1. NTSC DVDs of 'I Can't Think Straight' & 'The World Unseen'

2. Another award in Miami

3. Our upcoming screening in San Francisco

Well, I can feel you all falling about laughing already. I considered explaining to my wife that not everything in life can be reduced to bullet points, but I knew she would only have six reasons why it can be. So I kept quiet and started writing:

1. NTSC DVDs. When I first started being a writer I had lofty expectations of living in Paris, sucking down oysters and a crisp white wine, and doing nothing in between bouts at the typewriter but wrestling with existential angst and the meaning of life. In reality, I find myself wrestling with DVD formats. Part of the world is NTSC (North America, Japan, bits of South America) and most of the rest is PAL. Do you care? No. Should you care? If you want to watch Tala and Leyla making out on your TV and you live in Alaska or Tokyo, yes. You can get both formats now, from either film site, or www.enlightenment-productions.com.

2. We just won the Audience Award for 'I Can't Think Straight' at the Miami Gay & Lesbian Film Festival. We won the same award last year for 'The World Unseen', so there are no words to express how tasteful and brilliant I personally find all the lesbians of Miami. Hanan and I were there last year for the festival and they were so over sold that they actually screened the movie simultaneously in two cinemas. After which they threw us a beautiful dinner at a cool restaurant filled with women who looked like extras from 'The L Word'. Not a bad day at the office.

3. San Francisco GLFF (Frameline) just invited us to be at the screening of 'I Can't Think Straight' on June 22nd at the Castro. I missed last year ('The World

Unseen') because I was in Mumbai, finishing post-production on 'I Can't Think Straight'. That sounds a lot more glamorous than the reality, which was that I was being driven through Mumbai in the monsoon floods, with my prized final print of 'I Can't Think Straight' in the boot of the car. At this point, the car started filling up with water. I turned to Aseem Bajaj (my DP) and mentioned this. Or I may have shrieked and started jumping on the seats. 'The car's full of water'. 'I know,' he said, lifting a foot out of the pool gathering below us. 'That's why I wore flip flops'. 'But what about the film?' I whined. 'If it gets up to here,' he said, indicating his chin, 'we'll get out and carry it over our heads.' Obviously, I felt instantly reassured and there are still moments when I stop weeping at the thought of all my weeks in India and actually miss it, but it will be good to be slurping oysters and a dry white at Fisherman's Wharf in SF rather than dodging the swimming rats in Mumbai. Just for this once...

Proper attire for post production during the monsoon season in Mumbai, modelled by Enlightenment Employee of the Month for the 18th month running, Ms Aida Kattan

WHEN PIGS FLY...

May 14th

So TONIGHT WAS QUIZ NIGHT at our boys' school. It's hard to explain quite how much significance this charity evening has in the school social calendar. In terms of competition it makes the Tour de France look like a group of grannies out for a stroll. Raffle prizes and auction items are arranged from the finest companies in the country (of course Enlightenment Productions donated a set of 'I Can't Think Straight' and 'The World Unseen' DVDs and signed posters but there were a couple of other things too...) We all arrived, Hanan primed on her special quiz subjects ('Peace in the Middle East' and 'Complete Works of Beyonce and other Russian Pop Stars'). And then the headmaster stood up to make an announcement. We waited, impatiently. Was he going to ban Iphones (and cheating)? Would Stephen Hawking be removed from our table? Would we be allowed to Phone a Friend? No. Much worse than that, there were two cases of swine flu in the school. And quiz night was cancelled before it had even started.

Back at home, we checked our kids for temperatures (none), washed hands and donned surgical masks, then decided to hold our own Quiz Night over at our neighbour Kelly's house. The first question started out promisingly highbrow. Which three composers were born in the same year? But when Barry Manilow, Take That and Justin Timberlake were offered, I had an inkling that this might not be University Challenge exactly. This was confirmed by the next set of answers. 'Name one of the world's most dangerous races.' I know. Skiing at the Olympics, the Grand National, that sort of thing sprang to mind. "Arabs!' came the answer. And it was downhill from there, I'm afraid...

Quiz Night, and Shamim tries to remember if Marlon Brando was in 'The Godfather' or 'The Sound of Music', while Hanan waits happily for her question about Beyonce.

WIFE FOR SALE!
ONE CAREFUL, LADY OWNER…

May 16th

I SPENT THE MORNING trying not to whine that Hanan was nagging me to complete an email interview. I didn't succeed, but Hanan has an uncanny ability to tune out the sounds of my complaining and she continued to ask me if I'd finished the work every 30 minutes until I realised it would be better for my own sanity to just do it. It is this exact technique which makes her such an effective mother, not to mention film producer, and since I see from the romantic comments on Facebook that some of you are longing for your own Hanan, I suggested to her (after the 12th time she nagged me) that we should list her on www.enlightenment-productions.com as a 'Special Offer' alongside 'The World Unseen' and 'I Can't Think Straight' DVD and soundtrack packages. She suggested that instead of complaining to her, I should complain to my fans. So here it is. I don't mean a word of it, obviously, and I am also very aware that there is already a queue of women waiting for her, and the majority are younger, thinner and more French than me. So I will watch my back, or at least, Hanan's front.

We were at a birthday party for one of the boys' friends this afternoon, and as we sat with the school mums, the conversation naturally turned to clothes, shoes and (my personal favourite topic) make up. While I received a lesson in what to do with an Anti-Ageing Bronzer (polish the silverware? roast it for dinner?) I heard gasps of astonishment from the mothers clustered around Hanan. One may have hit the floor in a dead faint. I assumed that Hanan had been busy explaining the sex scene from 'I Can't Think Straight' again, but actually she had just revealed her true age. Which is…47 (next week). And no-one could believe it. I can tell you now, it ain't a bronzer or any foundation that makes her look so young. I don't think it is even having such a low maintenance wife (!) It's the genes. Which is why I'm not giving her up that easily. She is the apple of my eye. The rose upon my lips. And I'll go no lower anatomically…for now.

The beautiful Hanan Kattan. Just £19.99 plus postage and packing (and she only flies first class). Though for just £5.00 more you can get 2 DVDs and a Soundtrack instead!

ANGELS AND LESBIANS

May 19th

So WE JUST WENT to see 'Angels & Demons'. Why? Because it was at the cinema up the road and they have big seats and those chilli-flavoured crispy things and frankly, the idea of spending two hours sitting in the dark next to my wife felt slightly better than my alternatives of a) working and b) persuading my children not to make snorting noises through dinner. Also, I like to see what $100 million dollars gets spent on. Not so much on the script, sadly, but watching Tom Hanks find yet another angel statue with a sign on it saying 'Next Clue That Way!' gave me plenty of time to consider a rewrite of 'I Can't Think Straight' called...Angels and Lesbians, by Shamim Sarif. Or perhaps Lesbians and Demons. Anyway, it would begin when Tala and Leyla are called to Rome on an urgent mission by Hani, who has gotten over Tala jilting him at the altar by taking a vow of celibacy and becoming a priest in the Vatican. Our heroines then have to prevent Reema from crowning herself Pope, even as her cigarette starts spewing plumes of white smoke. Despite disguising Yasmin as a cardinal they are cruelly excluded from the corridors of power at every turn. After a brief interlude in a hotel room, dancing to 'Mambo Italiano' (have to keep that scene, right?), the pair fall through a trap door in the middle of the Trevi Fountain (where they had taken another break to participate in a Roman wet T shirt contest, which Tala was about to win), they race through underground tunnels and into a hidden crypt where they discover the housekeeper collecting vials of spit for the sole purpose of...but what am I doing?! If you want the rest of the story, you'll have to buy a movie ticket in 2010 like everyone else...

On the steps of the Vatican, Tala & Leyla prepare to rugby tackle the next cardinal who passes by.

THE DREAMING SPIRES…

May 26th

So LAST WEEK, Hanan decided we would go to Oxford for a recce for our next feature, 'The Dreaming Spires'. Generally, you do a location recce when you have most or all of the financing in place, but Hanan has a tattoo on her forehead which says 'Rules Are For Wimps' and she bundled me into the car together with Lou, who had been our line producer on 'I Can't Think Straight', and Aseem Bajaj, my stunning cinematographer on the same movie. I was excited to look at locations for the new movie, but as we roared up the motorway I began to get cold sweats because it took us all back to our previous film experience in Oxford for 'I Can't Think Straight', an experience that is now known as 'The Nightmare Spires'.

We were supposed to shoot in Paris, you see. That weekend between Tala and Leyla was all set for some glamorous shops and gourmet restaurants, and about 3 days before we were due to go, the then-financier announced that Paris was no longer an option. Wild-eyed, in the middle of a rough shoot, we all stared as he came up with a list of options closer to home. Cardiff. Blackpool. Maybe something even closer. Southall. Now I have no issue with Southall but it didn't have quite the same ring. Did you ever see Casablanca? 'We'll always have Paris.' I tried it in my mind. 'We'll always have Southall'. I turned to Hanan and started to weep. Anyway, after much scrambling, we hit on Oxford, which seemed to work as a place that appealed to Leyla, and somehow in 24 hours, Lou conjured up locations while Aseem and I and Hanan tried to hold the rest of the shoot together. We rocked up in Oxford late one night, a white van full of Indian crew tailing us, and a couple of bemused actors trying to learn new lines.

Our time there was a blur - I remember re-writing the script in a hotel room at 2am while our hair stylist set to work chopping off my hair (I complained every day, so she gave me a cut that she swore was funky, but which made me scare myself every time I glanced in a mirror). During our trophy shot in the beautiful Ashmolean Museum, I learned that the financier had driven off to London with all the film stock (probably selling it in Southall) leaving me enough to get that scene with only one take. And every time I shouted action during the picnic scene, the cows in the background started humping each other. Romantic comedy? It was a horror film.

'We'll always have Oxford…' Shamim and Hanan show Tala & Leyla how it's done.

IF THE CAFFEINE DOESN'T GET YOU, THE ANTI-OXIDENTS WILL

May 31st

My IDEA OF HEALTHY EATING is to throw a couple of raspberries onto my Coco Pops, so when Hanan left a couple of days ago to go to Vancouver, I felt myself drawn as if by gravity to the coffee, pasta and crisps...but in a rash moment of insanity, I had promised her to start being slightly healthier AND to tidy up my desk while she was away. She had a rough journey ahead to see a friend of ours who is very sick, so I thought the least I could do was stick to my end of the bargain.

It went incredibly well for the first 45 minutes. Then, I realised she was actually away for 4 days and began to get depressed. Nothing like a big plate of pasta for depression... but pasta is for Robert de Niro in The Godfather, not for me, whose body was a temple (OK, one of those crumbling but character-filled temples). Manfully, I threw the tagliatelle back into the cupboard and had some rice, fish and vegetables. Now I was still depressed, but feeling virtuous too which got me through the next hour. Then I went to sleep, which got me over a whole seven hours. This was getting easier. Next morning I cooked a fry up for the boys, and got myself a bowl of cereal. With fruit on it. The phone rang. It was Hanan. Having breakfast with Lisa Ray, star of 'The World Unseen' and 'I Can't Think Straight' (in case you'd forgotten) over in Vancouver. Lisa, I hasten to add, is not the sick friend, but she happens to be filming there and so they connected. This was all wonderful, but I had just turned down fried food for breakfast and my attempt at a yoga sun salutation was aborted by a flying child throwing himself at me like a little extra from Crouching Tiger. The virtuous feeling was gone.

Not to be put off, I hit the office, where I found piles of paper hurling themselves off the edge of my desk in a desperate and futile bid to be noticed and dealt with. This had been going on for some time, so I brought them all into one big pile and started to work on them from the top. The deeper I got, the more I could FEEL things festering in the middle. It was like a horror film. Every time I turned my back, something rustled on the desk behind me. I slid along the wall, stealthily, so the papers wouldn't see me. Across the street, the coffee shop beckoned...I grabbed my keys and headed for the door...You can't get through that kind of thing with a cup of green tea and an apple. It's not healthy.

Shamim realises that she forgot her Acai juice and protein shake at home…thank goodness there's a kebab shop around the corner from BAFTA…

BREAKFAST AT LISA'S

June 3rd

So WHILE I WAS RUNNING the office, looking after the kids, doing the shopping, organising the house and trying to write, Hanan was having breakfast with Lisa Ray. Here's a picture. Bitter? Moi? She deserves breakfast with beautiful women every morning, only I am not going to tell her that, because that can only go badly for me. Anyway, I digress. Hanan landed at Heathrow after her 12 hour flight from Vancouver and called me. What does Hanan say to you after a such a heart-wrenching absence, I hear you ask? 'I kissed the tarmac when I arrived on the soil that holds the love of my life'? Or: 'I found my existence in Canada meaningless because you weren't by my side?' Sort of. For a fraction of a moment, and then it went like this (as she went through passport control):

HK: 'Can you look up B-A-N-F-F or something online?'

SS: 'What?'

HK: 'It's a place in Canada. They have the biggest TV festival in the world. We keep talking about 'I Can't Think Straight' the TV series, we should do it.'

SS: 'When is this festival anyway?'

HK: 'Saturday. Oh, and can you find me a flight to Calgary that day?'

SS: 'I'm divorcing you.'

HK: 'Sure, but let me know about the flight, OK?'

Within 6 hours, Aida and I (OK, it was mostly Aida) had located this thing, registered, got flights, emailed all attendees and now I have 24 hours to write the treatment. I would get divorced but I don't have time...

Hanan has Lisa for breakfast. You know what I mean.

MOOSE HUNTING

June 9th

Why no blog, I hear you all ask (OK, 2 of you asked, and thank you). Because this week, after my wife jetted off to Calgary, I am a single, working mother. Frankly, it's not working for me. Having spent the best part of my adult life secretly believing that I did most of the work around here, I find myself drowning in a fraction of what Hanan manages to do. This includes almost anything to do with interacting with other people. So I have no idea what to do with our office interns. Luckily, Hanan has left them enough work to see them through to retirement, and they are diligent enough to get on with it, so I can go back to the school run - a big highlight for me, which starts with me standing, talking to myself on the street while I try to remember where I parked the car. Then, teeth gritted, I duel with other mothers for a parking spot and then realise I have forgotten to bring the kids their snacks.

'Mama never forgets our snacks,' the little one tells me. I buy him something with chocolate in it so he can't say anything else. Then home and a call from Hanan, up early to tap maple syrup from trees or whatever else she could possibly be doing in Canada at the Banff TV market.

'Good news, the broadcaster loves it. Needs a script'

'OK, I'll work on it this summer.'

'No they need it now. I told her you were putting the finishing touches on it.'

Resistant silence from Shamim.

'What, are you busy this week? Oh, and you need to apply for citizenship.'

So that's why I haven't blogged. I have been writing a TV script and becoming Canadian. I don't think Hanan and Aida are having meetings at all. I think they're out hunting moose. Or eating pancakes.

Hanan and Aida hunt down TV executives in Canada.

IN BRUGES…NO, ANTWERP, ACTUALLY

June 16th

THIS IS ABOUT LAST WEEKEND in Antwerp, but to get there we have to go back to February in London. This was when Hanan had the idea of doing a charity screening of 'The World Unseen'. She set a date at the end of March, emailed 1000 of her closest friends, then realised everyone was away for Easter and changed it to May. In the meantime, our friends Catalina and Chantal from Belgium (don't hold it against them, there is nothing boring about Belgium and I was there for 12 whole hours) had already BOOKED their flights and hotels, along with 2 friends. Naturally, completely mortified, we had them over to dinner that March night, where at the end of the main course and quite a lot of wine, Catalina announced that she had an 'indecent proposal' for us. Oh no, I remember thinking. Why does everyone think that lesbians swing from chandeliers? My idea of an indecent proposal is Hanan asking if I'd like to stop work at 10pm instead of midnight…Anyway, the proposal was that they had won a night in a movie theatre in Antwerp at a charity auction, and they wanted to screen 'The World Unseen'. We were overwhelmed by their generosity, and so relieved that there would be no attempted swapping of wives over dinner, that we accepted at once.

Cut to June, St Pancras Station. Remember when I felt sure I was going to be healthy? That I would be a lean, mean writing machine? Well, that lasted all the way up to the Eurostar terminal where we were meeting Leonie Casanova to get to Antwerp. My resolve weakened badly as I failed to pass by a foot-long sandwich at a French bakers, got even worse when an amazing fan, Annick, showered us with armfuls of Belgian chocolates and biscuits, and it died completely on an Antwerp street at 2 am with a beer in one hand and frites slathered in mayonnaise in the other. We staggered back to the hotel rooms that Catalina and Chantal had so generously arranged for us and lay on the very comfy bed to try and let some of the fat drain out of our arteries. I felt bad for about 5 minutes, then I remembered with relief that I was not put on this earth to make a health video. However, surviving C&C and their amazing hospitality is another challenge altogether…Leonie sang 'Broken' and 'Little Feeling' live, our charming hosts gave us a 10 minute tour of the city early on Saturday morning before our train home, and we got to see The World Unseen on a big screen again. When we got home we found that 'I Can't Think Straight' had won two more awards for Best Feature, one from Mallorca and the other from Calgary. That's what I call international appeal. In honour of which I invented a new recipe of Spanish tortilla with maple syrup. Don't. It can't be worse than it sounds. Can it?

Leonie, Hanan and Shamim keep their chocolates close, and their eyes on the crowd...

IT'S A FAIR COP, GUV

June 17th

JUST BACK FROM New Scotland Yard (Metropolitan Police HQ), where we were invited to be on a panel about LGBT hate crimes. Hanan agreed to this without consulting me, yet I got to sit up in front of 100 senior police personnel. That's a hate crime right there. Anyway, I learned many things by the end of this session:

1. Most policewomen do not look like Charlie's Angels

2. Domestic violence against lesbians includes mental abuse and frankly, I will be watching Hanan closely from now on

3. Bar charts and pie charts (even in colour) are no match for the trailer of 'I Can't Think Straight' for getting people's attention.

What can I do with this new-found knowledge, apart from be more vigilant about people making sarcastic comments about my flat shoes? We all agreed by the end that education is the key. I can be flippant about it here, but of course these crimes are too common and too real for many people. I hope that by getting emotionally involved with characters like Amina and Miriam, or Tala and Leyla, people realise that sexuality, colour and gender are the last things we should judge people on. It is, of course, perfectly acceptable to judge people if they voted for George W Bush or listen to Russian pop stars (except Beyonce). I am joking of course (sort of) but I felt a renewed energy to begin 'I Can't Think Straight 2', where Tala becomes a policewoman, handcuffs Reema and Kareem together, brings them to justice, then takes her handcuffs back home where Leyla is waiting with a pie chart showing how many people thought Lesbian food involved hummus and tabouleh...

Leyla makes a citizen's arrest.

I LEFT MY HEART IN SAN FRANCISCO

June 24th

I CAN'T BE FUNNY while jet-lagged. I just discovered this. Can't be funny, pluck my own eyebrows, or drive very well, while sleep-deprived. See? Anyway, this is about the trip to California. No words can describe the strangeness of switching from London (work and making children eat vegetables) to San Francisco (watching your own movie with 1500 people who laugh in all the right places). Screening at the Castro was the most fun I've had with my clothes on in ages. And how much more interactive Americans are than Brits! The sighs, the groans, the wolf whistles. And that was before the movie even started...The evening began with a book signing at A Different Light bookstore down the street. Things did not bode well when we showed up the morning of the signing to check on things, and the owner had no idea it was happening despite Aida's organising. Hastily, they printed a few flyers and stuck them on the door. Now, since the flyers were next to picture books filled with hunks of gay manhood, this did not fill me with confidence that anyone would actually show up. I shuffled in at 7.30 with a heavy heart and a direction from Hanan that we'd wrap it up in ten minutes...and found a roomful of lesbians of extremely good taste waiting expectantly. Quickly, I found a piece of 'I Can't Think Straight' to read out, and like any good writer, chose the part leading up to a sex scene and stopped right before it. I swear that helped sales...or maybe it was Sheetal who arrived as I finished, and also signed books (as herself, not me!) We met Hazel and Cecilia, the unofficial presidents of this fan page, and the screening was quite something. Thank you San Francisco, from Hanan, Aida and me, for one brilliant night.

Hanan, Sheetal and Shamim try to decide which movie to see outside the Castro…

THE DANCING SPIRES

July 1st

OCCASIONALLY, Hanan does some very odd things, and I don't mean just making us eat Middle Eastern okra or speaking fluent Japanese. A couple of days ago she got a lead to a Bollywood producer of mass market Indian movies, who swore he could make 'The Dreaming Spires' for less than the special offer pack of 'I Can't Think Straight' and 'The World Unseen'. Off she went to meet him.

HK: 'He thinks we can shoot 'The Dreaming Spires' in 15 days'

SS: 'He read the script?'

HK: 'No, but he said English films are half the length of Bollywood films, so...'

SS: 'Hanan, I can't shoot it in 2 weeks...'

HK: 'He said we would have to cut some of the songs and dancing to cut costs...'

SS: 'Songs? DANCING? Did you tell him it's not Bollywood?'

HK: 'I think you should consider it'

DIAL TONE AS SHAMIM HANGS UP

Postwar Oxford. Our English professor heroine Kate Graves is blinded from secret wartime heroism. And she has to sing 'I Can See Clearly Now' while cavorting by a fountain outside an Oxford college. Will you all excuse me? I have to go lie down.

Shamim and Hanan, with no budget for a choreographer, prepare to demonstrate the Bollywood dance number from 'The Dancing Spires'

THE HILLS ARE ALIVE

July 8th

WELL, YOU HAVEN'T LIVED till you have seen 'The Sound of Music' performed by 11 year olds as the end of term school play. My first thoughts were:

1. Thank goodness that Lisa Ray was not 11 years old when I directed her in 'The World Unseen' and:

2. I'm cured of my girlhood crush on Leisel Von Trapp forever.

Moving right along, Hanan is entreating me to spend more time on creative work, while simultaneously emailing me 1000 spreadsheets an hour to look at. Now that I am seriously trying to get into a writing state of mind, she seems more like a whirlwind than ever. I don't know how she does it. Even while she is out of the office at meetings, she texts, emails and psychically transmits ever-longer To Do lists for me and the small army of interns beavering away (don't take that the wrong way) in the office. But I cannot think about marketing and accounts. I am caught in a hazy no-man's land figuring out TV series plot-lines. Having analysed all these TV shows I am horrified, not to say exhausted, by how much happens in each one. I mean, should Tala lose her company, have an affair and go to jail all in the same episode? Can Leyla ditch Tala, join a convent, and escape Nazis before a commercial break?

Anyway, I digress. The point is, I am not doing well on the spreadsheet front and therefore not going to make Employee of the Month any time soon. No, that title is a toss up this month between Aida Kattan, our sari-wearing, LA-based miracle of productivity, and Esperanza, currently our longest-serving intern to date. I like to give any intern who lasts more than 3 months working for Hanan a medal and a small padded room to decompress in, but Esperanza, from Spain, has proven to be up to the job. And what does the Employee of the Month get, I hear you ask? Why, a free pair of 'I Can't Think Straight' panties of course. We may be cheap, but we ain't tacky...

Shamim tries to decide if Sheetal could be a singing nun in her upcoming remake of 'The Sound of Music'.

SLEEP IS FOR WIMPS

July 14th

I AM WRITING THIS at a time when I had hoped to be in bed, doing the thing that seems the most seductive, irresistible and pleasure-inducing. Yes, sleeping. But I am married to a woman who may soon need plastic surgery to have a Macbook removed from her hands. We left London a few days ago, grasping the opportunity to be in fresh air, and a bigger place for the school summer holidays. I don't know if you've ever been cooped up in a hot city apartment with two hyperactive boys, but I think it was banned as a torture option even in Guantanamo. So off we went, and I made my usual plea to Hanan to consider resting a bit - nothing as wild as taking a whole day off, mind you - maybe just stopping work at a normal time, and even reading a book or watching a movie after dinner. Just for a week or so. 'Sure,' she said. 'I was thinking about that myself'. Translated into the English that you and I understand, this actually means 'I was thinking about that and decided I would rather chew off my own head than take two hours off.' We go through the same routine every time we are away. It always ends with me threatening to go back to London (which she treats as the empty threat that it is) and eventually she sits down to watch TV with me. We haven't watched much since Cagney & Lacey used to sort out their problems in the bathroom and TV has gotten a lot faster, more realistic and suspenseful since then. I also spend half the time translating for Hanan what the cops are mumbling to each other. You know what? I'm going to bring her back her laptop, switch on some Russian pop music (!) and let her get on with it...especially since she is fire-fighting delays to the NTSC DVD shipments of 'I Can't Think Straight' and 'The World Unseen' from our distributor, which (as many of you are asking) really is a genuine manufacturing delay and really can't be helped. Trust me, if it could be done quicker, Hanan would find the way. Wait, I have to go. She's pressing DVDs herself...

Shamim's alter ego (as played by Sheetal Sheth) falls asleep at the crucial moment.

BEE MOVIE

July 15th

O<small>K</small>, so I am in BIG trouble and about to be kicked out of the house. What happened? Well, last night I was on the bed, finishing yesterday's blog, when a demented bee the size of a cow flew into the room. So, I had just finished criticizing my wife to 1000 Facebook fans, and now I needed her. You don't understand; I am more afraid of insects than of screening 'I Can't Think Straight' in Saudi Arabia. Hanan was still typing when I started screaming, ducking and generally behaving like someone under attack from a street gang. She looked up. She saw the bee. She saw the SIZE of it. And even she flinched. She leapt up, brandishing a Croc in one hand and a newspaper in the other. But this bee was mean and angry. We opened the window, switched off the lights (I say 'we' but it was her while I wept in the corner), but in the dark we couldn't see it zig zagging at head level around us. So I put on the bathroom light and cowered in the corner while my beloved duelled with this flying animal. And then it happened. The bee saw me. It grinned and flexed its muscles (I swear that's true) and came towards the bathroom light and me. And at the moment of truth, face to face with the enemy, with the chance to prove my heroism - I turned and ran and hid in the bathroom, leaving my wife flailing in the pitch dark with a killer bee. She got it in the end, with lightning reflexes, flipping it outside without killing it, thereby simultaneously stopping my whimpering and yet protecting her good karma. But then Hanan looked at me, with suspicion and horror.

'You left me alone in the pitch dark with a crazy bee,' she said.

'I panicked,' I muttered

'You saved yourself. You'd step on my head if I was drowning, wouldn't you?' she said.

I tried to explain that I would protect her from axe murderers, lunatics and film critics without a moment's hesitation, but when it came to insects, yes, I sold her down the river. It was a long night. And I still catch her looking at me narrowly. I failed my wife, cowed by a flying insect. I would make amends by sleeping outside tonight but I am too scared of the moths...

Can I really afford to alienate my wife…?!

PRINCESS OF PERSIA

July 18th

Well, WE JUST WATCHED ourselves online on BBC TV Persia. Yes, a big ole interview with pictures of our wedding, and clips of 'I Can't Think Straight' and 'The World Unseen', and Leyla and Tala making out were just broadcast to 8 million people in Iran, a country not known for its gay pride festivals. This warms the cockles of my heart, even while I know we can cross Tehran off our potential holiday destinations for a while to come. I can't tell how the interview came out because we were dubbed in Farsi. Hanan got a sexy female voice which sounded like the Iranian Angelina Jolie, and I did not. No matter, she deserves husky Persian women after the bee incident.

In other news, my sister arrived in Switzerland to look after the children while we head off to Oxford and the TED Global conference this week. For us, it's the first time we attend a high-octane group of guest speakers over 4 days who have 18 minutes each to talk about their own passions, ideas, research etc. For my sister with our boys, it's the best contraceptive ever invented. She is a gem, giving us the time to make trips like this, and ahead of her nights in with kids, we are going out tonight to the village restaurant. Now this place is great, if a little rustic, but 10 minutes in the other direction, Prince is playing at the Montreux Jazz Festival. There are no tickets to be had but I gave Hanan the theoretical choice - the Purple One ('Is he Russian?' she asked) or dinner in the village. She hates crowds, and couldn't remember more than one Prince song, so she chose the village. I guess we're even on the bee incident after all...

Hanan, deep undercover following her appearance on Iranian TV, can't help continuing to promote the films...

TEDDY GIRLS

July 24th

So, DID you miss me?! Yes, we're back from TED Global, having spent a riotous few days immersed in nuclear physics, quantum mechanics, environmental issues and too much wine. The wine was necessary in order to understand half the talks, and I for one was MUCH clearer about parallel universes after two glasses of French burgundy. But I was not clear about how it was that in the bathroom breaks I bumped into lovely people, but always mathematicians or conservationists (nothing wrong with either obviously) while Hanan bumped into Cameron Diaz. You see, Hanan definitely lives in a parallel universe to me, where we are together until stunningly good-looking actresses are around, and I am somehow swallowed into a black hole. Anyway, I digress. It was not all mind-blowing, but quite a bit was, and it felt like a big privilege to be able to focus just on soaking up all this amazing cutting edge research that people are doing. And we met at least one person who I think will be a life-long friend, and as a professional hermit, I don't say that often. What was interesting was that, by and large, the arts and entertainment side of things were used as an interlude, which was great but I'd like to see the artistic process and the power of the arts to move people examined and discussed more. The talks that excited people the most were the ones that stimulated the emotions and not just the mind. On that front, we were all left a mess by the story of Emmanuel Jal, whose mother was murdered when he was 7, leaving him to be recruited as a child soldier at the age of 8 before he was rescued after nearly starving to death, and smuggled out of Sudan by a courageous aid worker, and is now a music artist. Anyway, I just wanted to cheer you all up! Listen, I promise the next blog will be funnier, OK?

Hanan and Shamim in Oxford. The huge name tag is for the next time I fall into a parallel universe...

HANAN TAKES OVER THE BLOG

July 28th

Hello Shamim's fans. Hanan here.

Yes I don't use FB (emails are high tech enough for me and take too much time) but I decided to say hello, to say a few things and to share new links with you of a recent interview with Shamim that Aida, my baby sister, sent me last night from LA.

I want to start by saying 'thank you' for your incredible support and help in supporting our work and in spreading the word. It is so much appreciated at many levels.

After thirteen wonderful & tough years together (mainly due to family drama), Shamim remains the love of my life and there are not enough words to describe how I feel about her (it is handy that there is one writer in the family who is eloquent). Yes, she nags and complains that I don't give her a break but do you blame me?? She is such a talented and brilliant novelist, script writer, film director and songwriter that it would be a travesty if she did not spend more of her time on creating incredible work that inspires, moves and motivates while entertaining.

Like most creative artists, she can drift (that is my excuse) and needs focus (of course she disagrees) and I normally let her go on complaining (while I switch off) and when she finishes I am onto the next thing asking her when will she have her first draft ready (by which time she is ready to throw me out of the window – luckily we live on the first floor).

As a first time director, she has created two amazing features films that are different genres - 'The World Unseen' which is a period piece and 'I Can't Think Straight', a contemporary romantic comedy, and she switched the roles of the extroverted Tala to Miriam and the introverted Leyla to Amina in both films which shows her incredible depth and range in directing. And choosing actresses who could rise to the challenge so elegantly and beautifully is a talent in itself.

I am not sure if any of you have been on a movie set or know what it takes to produce and direct a movie (if you watch some of the videos on our Enlightenment Productions channel, you will get a glimpse of the behind the scenes of making a movie). One has to be passionate and a bit mad to do what we do but it is a satisfying and thrilling process despite the stresses, the long hours and the sleepless nights. And we are glad that you all have the good taste to enjoy the end result.

Besides Shamim's brilliance with films and novels, she is a wonderful cook and makes sinful and orgasmic deserts (not good on the weight front), she plays the piano beautifully (if she only had more time to play), she is an amazing mother to our two boys (and does all the homework with them), she is much better than I am in finance and numbers (it comes in handy when shooting a film to stay on budget) and she is an amazing partner and wife and she makes me laugh a lot with her sense of humour (which you have all enjoyed in her various work).

Ok, so can one person be so perfect you ask? Besides her mood swings (which I excuse due to her artistic temperament), her introverted hermit-like existence (as she prefers being alone creating than mixing with people), living in her head half the time creating stories and characters (yes, it can get lonely), getting grouchy if she has to sleep late (ie past 10 pm) and her jealousy thinking that every woman who looks at me falls for me (clearly she is still in love or blind and I remind her that even though she had me up for sale, I did not get one bid!), Shamim is the most amazing partner I can ask for and when she starts complaining, I tell her to go complain to her fans as I am too busy (which I normally am). So thank you for dealing with her complaints when she is venting.

So, Shamim's fans, thank you for your support and for enjoying her blogs (which make me laugh when I read them even though I am the punching bag). And this time I get to choose a picture for her blog - from our wedding.

Here are the links to the interview; enjoy and please share with your friends and maybe translate if you have time into your local language and pass on.

Thanks again. Hanan

http://www.cherrygrrl.com/renaissance-woman-shamim-sarif/

http://www.cherrygrrl.com/lesbian-fiction-perfected-in-%25E2%2580%259Ci-can%25E2%2580%2599t-think-straight/

Shamim ready to throw me in the river...(!) She didn't want to share this photo, but the producer has taken over for today.

THE WEDDING CRASHERS

July 30th

I'M BACK! Three days ago I was hijacked while walking up the hill from the Swiss village nearest us, clutching my paper bag of croissants ('never walk long distances without carbs' is on the Sarif family's coat of arms). A woman with suspiciously curly hair and a sexy Arabic accent attacked me with a Macbook, and the last thing I remember as I lost consciousness with a croissant stuffed into my mouth, was that she was asking for my Facebook password...Well, I am glad you all bonded while I was script writing, but I have to tell you, that photo of our wedding day reminded me that ONLY my wife could have proposed getting married right in the middle of pre-production on 'I Can't Think Straight'. Yes, not only were we desperately finding crew, locations and Eastern women who could act and also consent to lesbian love scenes, but we were also planning a wedding! And this was how it went:

HK: 'Let's get married now.'

SS: 'I can't think about marriage. I can't think about anything except I Can't Think Straight.'

HK: 'It'll be a piece of cake.'

I don't know how she persuades me into these hair-brained schemes but I actually MADE the wedding cake (yes, I am a sucker) in between rewriting the script and drawing up shot lists. Our costume designer made our wedding outfits between sourcing clothes for Tala and Leyla. By the time the day arrived, I had no idea if I was shooting a wedding or marrying a film. I begged for a honeymoon but suddenly I didn't have a wife, I had a producer, and I had to go back to auditioning actresses (why do I sense you're not feeling that sorry for me?!)

Would I do it all again? In a heartbeat. The only thing better than marrying a real-life Tala is casting the pretend one at the same time, right..?

Hanan and Shamim run past their unsuspecting wedding guests and straight onto the set of 'I Can't Think Straight.'

SHAMIM SARIF

PIRATES OF THE CAPPUCCINO

August 1st 2009

THIRTEEN YEARS LATER, I've finally discovered the way to send Hanan insane with pleasure. But before you feel sorry for her 13 year drought, you should understand that all I did was make her the perfect cappuccino. So what, you might ask? We live in a frappacino world, baby. But Hanan is someone who, when ordering coffee (or anything else for that matter) makes Meg Ryan in 'When Harry Met Sally' look decisive. Her cappuccino has to be like me after a long day's writing – weak and skinny (I wish). And it has to have a lot of foam and then just a sprinkle of brown sugar and a dusting of chocolate. You can imagine how that request goes down in a stolid Swiss village tea room. Like a bucket of cold fondue.

So I armed myself with this vibrating instrument (get your minds out of the gutter) that makes milk froth, and set to work creating a perfect cappuccino at home. On the plus side, it worked, and my wife thinks I am a genius. On the down side, that's three hours of my day gone brewing, frothing, sprinkling and shaking. When I look back and ask myself why I never won the Nobel Prize for Literature, I can say, at least I made the perfect cappuccino.

Anyway, this is not the point of the blog and, as usual, I digress. What I wanted to tell you is that we were in the sole Indian shop in this Swiss town (yes, there is one, open all hours, and yes, we found it!) buying lime pickle and basmati rice, when we saw a pile of Hindi DVDs. The Indian shopkeeper saw an opportunity and rushed over to plug them.

'Only 10 francs, Madam.'

'No, I don't do Bollywood, thanks' I said snootily.

'Want English Hindi fillum, Madam?' he asked and before I could wonder what an English Hindi 'fillum' could possibly be, I swear to you, he whipped out a PI-RATED copy of 'The World Unseen'. Complete with disgusting cover with Lisa's face touched up with more Bollywood-style makeup.

I said 'Hey, that's my film!' He didn't understand. So I shouted (I was upset) 'This DVD is MY fillum!'. 'Yes, madam,' he said. 'For 10 francs this is YOUR fillum...'

I gave up and paid him the 10 francs.

I couldn't believe it. In the Swiss Alps, we found our first pirated copy. I took a picture of Hanan holding it (below). When we got home, I put it in the player. It came up with a menu for subtitle and SONGS. I clicked with trepidation, trying to prepare mentally for Amina to come flying out of the café singing 'It's Raining Women, Halleljuah!'. Luckily the song menu was blank. But the rest of it wasn't. I'm depressed frankly. Though on the plus side, the front of this copy told us that we'd won the Toronto Film Festival, which frankly, was news to us. We found out a Hong Kong company called Applewood is manufacturing DVDs by the millions. Find them, my fans. And exterminate. In the meantime, we're teaming with a company in Belgium and Netherlands to intercept this stuff, so if you see any of these copies, let us know. Your director and producer need you. Or we'll have to go work in a coffee bar…

The agony and the ecstasy…not even a perfect cappuccino can make a pirated DVD palatable…

I CAN'T THINK STRAIGHT…
AND I CAN'T HEAR A THING!

August 5th

So I'VE FINISHED the pilot episode of 'I Can't Think Straight' the TV show. There is no better feeling in the world than finishing a piece of writing. OK, there is one better feeling, but I'm not going into that here, you catch my drift. But I'll tell you what, figuring out an hour's worth of drama for 13 consecutive episodes is exhausting (and a lot of fun). Being a quiet girl from Surrey, I had trouble coming up with enough drama, insanity and plot. Being a feisty world citizen from Palestine, Hanan had trouble toning all her drama down. She just had to go back about 6 months into her family's history…anyway, I digress. As we went for a mid-morning swim to celebrate (absolutely unheard of for Hanan to take half an hour off in the day, even here in Switzerland, and I still suspect there's going to be a downside, like rewriting all night) we were thinking back to everything we've been through getting the movie of 'I Can't Think Straight' to the screen. Frankly, there's enough there for 30 blogs, but what most people don't realise is one of our biggest challenges (other than losing the movie, spending 18 months chasing it through courts, and getting it back) was that we never got back the sound.

Sure you did, I hear you cry. We can hear Tala and Leyla panting just fine. Well, it was all recreated from scratch. Forgive me if I am telling you stuff you already know, but when you shoot a film, you shoot the picture on film and the sound on tape and the two are synced for editing, but don't actually meet again till you make the final print. So we got back the film itself, but the sound was gone, held hostage by the crooked first investor.

Sadly, this meant a lot of dubbing. That meant every actor coming into a studio with me and re-recording their lines in sync with the existing film picture. And giving a good performance. Yes, this involved being in a small darkened room with Lisa Ray for a week but it was hard work, trust me! After a while, it's like a bizarre Groundhog Day. Every day you get up, schlep to the studio, drink coffee, eat the pastries they have lying around and try and direct the film again in the dark with one actor.

The thing I loved about Lisa on set was that every take of a single line would be different, and often with subtle changes to the line. But we didn't love it so much as we stared at the screen trying to decide what she was saying to Leyla. And then every background sound, touch, rustle of clothing and atmosphere had to be added (foleys and effects). And all mixed together. There's only one thing worse than doing sound mixing from scratch, and that is doing sound mixing from scratch in Mumbai. Overdosed on daal, I spent long nights (why does everyone work all night in India?) trying to match sync to a picture that was out of focus...before Hanan managed to get a deal from Pinewood Studios to finish the mix.

I loved many things about India, but going from there to Pinewood was like going from - how do I put this - Lamia to Tala. There's a difference in sensibility. They were shooting the last couple of days of the Bond film, and next door, with the same mixers, was a small movie called 'Slumdog Millionaire'. I hope it did OK...

Lisa Ray tries to convince Shamim that 'I Can't Think Straight' should be a silent movie...

THE L-WORD IS FOR LUCKY

August 8th

W AS WATCHING AN EPISODE or two of 'The L Word' the other night - purely for work purposes, you understand, studying structure and all that, and I completely ignored all the gratuitous sex (by which time the episode was over) - but it did remind me that we had thought about Sarah Shahi ('Carmen') for the role of Leyla, just after we cast Lisa Ray and were still looking for someone for her to fall in love with...Anyway, we sent her the script and she loved it, but was worried about being typecast and was tired of lesbian sex. I know, how is such a thing possible? But I guess day in, day out panting and writhing on 'The L Word' would make anyone beg to keep their clothes on and just watch the food channel with a cup of tea. She was good enough to call me and explain all this, and I think it probably didn't help that Hanan and I had not one film industry credit to our names (and had never been on a film set, not that I rushed to mention that on the phone with Sarah) and doing 'I Can't Think Straight' would have meant her flying to London to be with people she didn't know and no-one in LA had ever heard of. I am SURE she regrets it now :) but no matter, we found our Leyla in the end and maybe Sarah would do something in the TV version of 'I Can't Think Straight', should it get off the ground. Ideas for her role? In the meantime, I have to risk being asked to give up my After Ellen International Lesbian of the Year Award because I have done what no self-respecting lesbian would ever do - I actually had Carmen's mobile phone number and lost it.

In other news, Aida (who perhaps has a tad too much time on her hands right now) suggests that I come up with some alternative uses for the extra PAL DVD of 'I Can't Think Straight' that some of you ended up with due to a factory error. I've been told that the problem is solved, and that special packages are now in beautiful new slip cases (ideal for gifts! Hanan says). In the meantime, Aida says you can play frisbee with the spare DVD. It also makes a handy coaster for hot drinks, and two of them would be great earrings that would certainly make a statement (even if the statement is 'I am bored AND tasteless') - and if you string twelve together you have your own funky ICTS necklace that is even cooler than the pink silicone bracelet in your pack. Please don't thank us, multi-tasking and multi-use is what we do here at Enlightenment. Even Lisa and Sheetal played two characters each, right?!

On the set of 'The World Unseen', Lisa, Sheetal and Natalie can't believe what Shamim can do with a spare DVD…

SILENCE OF THE LAMBS

August 12th

REMEMBER THE SHORT POST about our dinner at the Swiss neighbours? Why would you, it was like, 30 posts ago, and while I know certain of you know the entire script of 'I Can't Think Straight' by heart, and others know exactly how many times Lisa Ray sighs in 'The World Unseen', I am sure you haven't committed every blog to memory just yet. I digress, as usual. My point is, tonight was payback time and we had them over to our place. I was under instructions to make it quick which worked for me, the hermit of the family. I asked Hanan if I should just meet them at the door with the roast chicken, but she drew the line there. Well, I learned many things this evening:

1. Even discussing local garbage regulations in French sounds sexy (when Hanan does it, not the neighbours)

2. One should never try to use British irony, especially when communicating in school girl French. When they asked what I thought of the sheep that are grazing at the end of our garden, I said (tried to say) they made me feel hungry. There was a horrible silence during which I felt like Hannibal Lecter and we could only hear the little tinkling bells around the lambs' necks.

3. One should not look directly at a yawning man who wears dentures, especially loose dentures.

Anyway, you get the gist. On the plus side, for once time did not seem to fly. In fact it sort of dragged. Till the conversation about supermarkets, then time just stood still. But they left, and now I have a moment to write this before crashing. I was up late last night, grilling Hanan about her five ex-fiances. I get them mixed up, especially since many came around the block more than once. Once in a while I like to remind myself of the order and the cause of the break up, even though it leaves me broken out in an icy sweat as I realise I have married the original runaway bride. But more of the break-ups later. Enough drama there to make Richard Burton and Elizabeth Taylor look like a couple of Swiss neighbours...

Shamim looking for kebabs for dinner. (Check the background, you'll see them!)

HIKING WITH HANAN

August 15th

We SPENT THE DAY hiking the other day. Ah, the smell of wild grass and Swiss wildflowers, a chance to discover 'The World Unseen' for real, the pungent aroma of cow dung and and delicate scent of...croissants. Yes, folks, this was no ordinary hike. Backpacks and dried fruit are so 'last decade'. We hiked (as we do everything where Hanan is involved) with style and with real food. It began when we dropped off the boys for a day at summer camp. We dropped them right by a bakery and it would have been churlish not to buy pain au chocolat, so we did. I re-gretted inhaling these as soon as we began a wild ride up the mountain in a vehicle the size of Texas. Why do they make cars so big in a country with such small roads? Hanan's habit of fiddling while driving (with the radio, with a nail file, with packets of sweets) is sometimes endearing, sometimes admirable (how does she unwrap sweets, change CDs, make a list and drive all at once?) but on hairpin mountain bends it is simply terrifying.

However, we arrived, in one piece, and parked up at a little restaurant at the top. I jumped out, ready to set off up the trail towards our date with Mother Na-ture. 'Shall we have a hot chocolate first? Since we're here?' Hanan asked. We sat and snorted liquid chocolate which helped ease the motion sickness nicely. And then we set off. Three and a half minutes into the hike, Hanan stopped and took off her (our) backpack. 'We should re-hydrate' she advised, whipping out a bottle of Evian. We re-hydrated. Two minutes later, she stopped again, to re-apply sun-block.

'Isn't this a little excessive?' I ventured.

'Do you want to be married to someone with wrinkles like chasms?'

'Er...no. I mean, yes. I mean, I don't mind either way.'

I decided to keep quiet and just hike. When my wife was ready. Off we went again. After twenty minutes (and three more water breaks) we reached a tiny vil-lage with 15 chalets, no electricity but one (you guessed it) restaurant.

'All this exercise is making me hungry,' Hanan said.

All this exercise? I was wishing I'd gone for a run before we'd left. I'd had more exercise flicking channels on TV. This must be what it's like hiking in Beverley Hills or Mayfair. We stopped. Hanan ordered a cappuccino and a croissant and was met by blank stares. There was only one breakfast and it was 4 slabs of bread, 2 slabs of butter, 2 hunks of Swiss cheese and a trough of homemade jam. We hiked on, for a full 30 minutes and then Hanan started looking for shade and a place to sit down. We sat and I watched with misgiving as she started rummaging in the backpack. I was sure she had firewood, matches and a spit-ready chicken in there. But no, out came an ominously large wad of paper and two pens. I tried not to look alarmed.

'I thought this would be a good place to do our goals', she said.

Goals? I thought. My goal is to walk fast enough to get my heart rate past that of a ninety-year-old's. But, alas, that was not what she meant. So we sat and wrote out our goals for the year. I left out 'taking Sundays off' as I didn't want to antagonise a woman who hadn't eaten for 15 minutes...finally, we were done. Our first goals were remarkably similar. To lose weight and get fitter. With that in mind, we hiked the 20 minutes back to the same (the only) restaurant, and just asked for 'lunch'. Up came plates of rosti (grated, fried potatoes) layered with bacon and slathered with melted cheese. Hanan looked at me.
'What about our goal?' she asked.

'Let's start tomorrow.' I said and tucked in...

Shamim in her last moments before being eaten by Hanan after a gruelling 25 minute hike...

ON SET ON 'THE WORLD UNSEEN'

August 21st

IN THE 'PRODUCER'S GUIDE to Low Budget Filmmaking', written by Hanan Kattan (don't rush to Amazon, she hasn't had time to actually write it yet) there are two main requirements:

1. Seduce the writer and director (if they are one and the same, like Shamim Sarif, it saves time and a candlelight dinner)

2. Employ your children and pay them in South African rands so they think they're being paid handsomely.

Which is how Ethan, our eldest, came to be on 'The World Unseen' set, having breakfast at 5am with Lisa Ray. Between mouthfuls of baked beans, he asked her how much she was making on the film. Lisa arched an eyebrow and advised him to get an agent. But by then it was too late, the contracts were signed and he was being paid a pittance to be attacked by South African cops. Now you can't find a more charming pair than Colin Moss and Rod Priestley, who played the policemen in 'The World Unseen'. But I'd asked them to keep a distance from the kids, so Ethan was a little nervous of them by the time that scene came around. I had also had the camera movement rehearsed without the kids, so when we shot handheld, it might be fresh. Well, fresh it was. The camera rolled, I yelled 'Action' and they grabbed the kids, and gave Ethan cuts on his arms while hustling him into the police van. Ethan finished the take, turned to me and burst into tears, terrified. We took him to the side, comforted him, and held him.

'I'm not doing that again!' he cried.

Faced with that choice - my petrified, imploring child, or getting the right take..I chose the take.

'You're back on in 5, kid,' I said. Well, not exactly, but you get the drift. And he did it twice more with Hanan calculating future therapy bills over my shoulder. I should say that when he isn't being brutalised by police, Ethan and his brother Luca are more known for never hesitating to argue, resist bedtimes or be selectively deaf when their mommies are addressing them. So I thought Luca would have no problem playing Miriam's cheeky nephew (the one who sticks his tongue out early on). Another cast salary saved...and I must say that their acting has only continued to improve, as just yesterday they swore blind that they'd tidied their room and I walked in to find it looking like hungry looters had passed through.

They may not have made their fortunes yet, but you can't put a price on being Lisa Ray's son for a while, frankly, or on being baby sat by Leonie Casanova (she's still recovering but the therapists say her new phobia of children will pass). True, Luca lost a tooth in a pillow fight with Lisa Ray, but they think it's completely normal to see Aunty Lisa at the movies, or hear Aunty Leonie sing 'Broken' on the CD player. They were also the kids in the park in the last scene of I Can't Think Straight (a movie which took employing family and friends in cameos to new heights). Immortalised on film forever… In fact, I may actually send them an invoice…

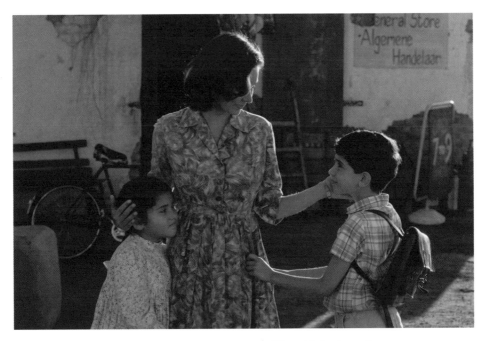

Ethan asks Lisa if he can come and live with her instead…

'I CAN'T THINK STRAIGHT' GOES STRAIGHT

August 24th

So 'I CAN'T THINK STRAIGHT' opens theatrically in India on 11th September. The idea of 'Leesa Ray' as a lesbian sent everyone into a tailspin on the subcontinent even when we cast her, so I can't wait to see what happens now. First up, it's been rated 'A' - I was thrilled, as everyone likes to get an A grade for their creative genius - but Hanan quickly explained it was for 'Adults Only'. Within a moment I went from feeling like the new Scorsese to feeling like I'd inadvertently made a porn film. It gets worse. The Indian censors cut the film. Which part, you cry? Did they disagree that life insurance sells itself? Did they take exception to Maya forbidding Yasmin to backpack 'in India of all places'? Or could it possibly, perhaps, maybe be that they chopped my tasteful sex scene (yes, the 2nd one apparently) to smithereens? Reader, they did. Well, I can hear you all gasping from here. Which is just as well, as we certainly won't be hearing Lisa or Sheetal panting over there. Never mind, we will just drive around Mumbai and sell the real DVDs (with 'extra sex scene!') out of the back of an auto-rickshaw...

In other news, things in sleepy Switzerland have been shaken up recently, with the arrival of some of Hanan's family staying in the house attached to the one we're in (which belongs to her dad, it's all very complicated). They've been a blast, and with the intense heat pulling the Palestinian Jordanians, the Pakistan/Canadian neighbours, and us out in the evenings, it's all like a much greener version of downtown Lahore or Amman. Loving it. The sheep are loving it somewhat less, and I swear, when the Arabs fired up the barbecue, those sheep sensed a shawarma in their near future and they RAN - faster than a Mumbai censor.

'I'm sorry, Leyla, I can't kiss you. Not here in Bangalore. But we'll always have Oxford...'

LESBIANS IN QUICKSAND

August 28th

So ETHAN WOKE ME UP this morning with an idea for a movie.

'Not those lesbian-type movies you make now like 'The World Unseen' but a kid's movie!'

'A lesbian kids movie?' I mumbled, half-asleep. Before he could launch into Act 3 of his storyline (involving scary men disappearing into quicksand) I fled the house in search of a quiet place where I could write without interruption, maybe a Hemingway-esque cafe where I could nurse a drink and think great thoughts. I ended up in the local bakery. Where Papa Hemingway looked up from his Chablis and saw chic young Parisian girls across the room, I had Swiss matrons when I glanced up from my coffee, but I was determined not to lose the moment - that is, until the background music came into aural focus. Why do Swiss tearooms always play the greatest hits from 1983? I love Bonnie Tyler as much as the next lesbian but, you know, there are only so many total eclipses of the heart you can stand before you have to pack up and go home.

Back at the homestead, I found that while I had been opening my heart and soul to plumb the depths of the human psyche in search of a rare glimpse of truth (ie, while I had been writing a page of a script), Hanan had taken a break from marketing 'I Can't Think Straight' to email an ex-boyfriend who had tracked her down out of the blue. Worse, this was not even one of the 5 ex-fiances, this was an 'over and above' boyfriend.

'Arab?' I asked, trying to be conversational.

'German,' she answered.

'Hmm. Ugly?' (My conversational capacity is limited when it comes to chewing the fat over exes)

'Stunningly handsome,' she said. 'Blue eyes, broad chest, tall, muscles..'

All right, okay, I had the picture. And he'd sent another, an update from 30 years ago when he had met Hanan at hotel school here in Switzerland. Yes, you read that right. Hanan was at hotel school for about 30 minutes, many moons ago. She made it through the Patisserie course, only to break out of the campus when it came to

Butchery, realising that her true lot in life was to stay at Ritz-Carltons, not run them. I wondered if perhaps Herr Hotel School had put on weight, perhaps lost all his hair. But no, he looked pretty good. I called for Ethan to tell me how that quicksand worked again, but he wasn't interested any more. You know, I think I should just just run back down to the bakery, pick up some cakes and borrow that Pet Shop Boys CD, and invite all the exes over in one go. What a blog that would be...

'Sheetal, I heard Shamim wants us to wrestle in quicksand, while listening to Bonnie Tyler.'
'No, I think it was Julio Iglesias.'

SAGGING BOSOM SEEKS UPLIFT!

August 30th

OK, I NEED TO START by saying that - despite the snappy title - this is not meant to be a funny blog. I have not spent the day nit-picking Hanan's behaviour (well, I have) but not so I can complain to you now. Instead, I bring you exciting news on the marketing front which is that one of our fans Zelia Hagiwara - yes, the very same fan who offered me her sagging bosom to rest my weary head upon - has kindly offered to spearhead the online marketing efforts for 'The World Unseen' and 'I Can't Think Straight' films, books & music.

Zelia will be working closely with Hanan & myself but not so closely that we can tell if her booty is really drooping or not. I suspect that secretly, she looks like Beyonce. In fact, she may actually BE Beyonce for all I know, and I will have Hanan drop her a little email in Russian to check.

But, I digress. Zelia would appreciate any help from fans who are willing to put in a bit of free time in a grassroots efforts to help sales and awareness. Any motivated fans who have the time to support, please contact Zelia directly on her e-mail below and DO NOT pester her about her bosom, ok?

zelialobohagiwara@yahoo.com

Need motivation? Just think of I Can't Think Straight 2 (featuring 6 love scenes) and The World Unseen 2 - Omar's Revenge. These tasteful and life-changing films can only be brought to you if we can repay the women who invested in us for these films.

Need time? Then stop reading this and email Zelia!

Need a bosom to cry on? Email Zelia!

So many of you have done a ton of amazing work, and continue to do so, and you know who you are so I won't name even the most brilliant of you, Sariena Carmichael (oops). Sariena continues to single-handedly hunt down anyone who has ever THOUGHT of illegally downloading and elegantly persuade them not to, while simultaneously marketing (and the next announcement will be one of her brilliant ideas). What have I done to deserve such wonderful supporters? (That's rhetorical, I ain't fishing for compliments). I'm going to go now, and see if my own Beyonce impersonation will lure Hanan away from her Macbook. Hold on....
OK, I'm back. And it didn't. Sigh.

Zelia Hagiwara and Sariena Carmichael contemplate the best way to sell lots of DVDs.

LISA RAY

September 3rd

I WILL CUT MY HAIR like Julie Andrews in 'The Sound of Music', I will hug a cow, I will wear lederhosen, or all three of the above. Just get me back to Switzerland. Yes, in the grey light of London, I bitterly regret every snipe I ever made about cuckoo clocks and boring neighbours. Having spent two arduous hours buying school shoes (you queue for an hour to get served, then you argue with your child who wants the red, flashy, EXPENSIVE football boots, then you get fitted by an assistant who lost the will to live three days before, give in to the child, go home and get asked by your wife what you were doing all afternoon) I am ready for a life of self-imposed solitude by a Swiss lake. I don't care if I have to listen to 'Total Eclipse of the Heart' for the rest of my life in the tearoom.

However, every cloud has a silver lining, or as they say in the Middle East, every bleating lamb can make a good kebab (before you all go up in arms, I don't think anyone in the Middle East ever said that, but I'm struggling for metaphors amid the school runs, homework and office so give me a break OK?) And the silver lining for me was that Lisa Ray sent me the link to her new website. In fact, I think it's her first ever website. I was a bit annoyed, frankly, when I found that she'd used that photo for the home page, because I had just taken photos of myself lying back, with my hand in my long mane of hair, staring smoulderingly at the camera, and was going to use that for MY site, but it's too late now. Other than that, I love this site. And not just because it has photos of Lisa on it. It's clean, lean, contemporary, sexy. Just like Lisa herself. And if that isn't enough, she has a quote from poet ee cummings on there. What more do you want? Spread a little happiness to everyone you know and pass this link along...http://www.lisaraniray.com/

Lisa Ray asks Shamim to stop copying her website photos…

YOUR TURN TO MAKE THE MOVIES

September 6th

WELL, THE ONLY THING better than watching Lisa Ray and Sheetal Sheth play Tala and Leyla or Amina and Miriam, is watching them do it in slow motion. I discovered this truth a few months ago when I innocently visited YouTube to check out the Enlightenment Productions channel (how kind of you to ask, it's http://www.youtube.com/user/EnlightenmentProds) and up popped that 'Related Videos You Might Like' window on the side. Hmm, I thought deeply as I scrolled down. 'Sheetal Sheth kiss!' was one title. Been there, directed that. I moved on. And there they were. Hundreds of 'Lisa & Sheetal', 'Tala & Leyla', 'Amina & Miriam' videos. The lists went on and on, and I found myself compulsively clicking at random to find slow motion love scenes set to Bryan Adams. And then a slow motion love scene set to Celine Dion (moved on quickly from that, forgive me). And a slow motion love scene set...you get the picture. Maybe you MADE the picture. And if you did, or if you think you can do better, then you are in luck. With the advice of Sariena Carmichael, formerly a fan, now unofficial Head of Marketing at Enlightenment Headquarters (I like that idea, don't you? EP HQ! We could have holograms of Lisa and Sheetal everywhere, and compulsory wine breaks every hour) we are about to launch our first ever competition to make a fan video, from scenes from 'I Can't Think Straight' or 'The World Unseen' or both, if you have incredible stamina and the ability to stay conscious when faced with a double dose of Lisa and Sheetal. There are rules, and while we at Enlightenment know that rules are made to be broken, these ones should be adhered to. They'll be up on our website (www.enlightenment-productions.com, like you didn't know that) tomorrow. And better than that, Hanan and I are starring in our own three minute video to introduce the competition which will be on the EP site and on this page, if our video-maker Esperanza - former 'employee of the month' - can overcome what she herself acknowledges as an addiction to Spanish time, which means she is 2 days behind every deadline. It took every ounce of self-will for Hanan and I not to recreate the love scenes in slow motion, but in the end, we decided that we love and appreciate you all, and couldn't put you through it. You can thank us later.

Shamim explains to Sheetal that 'The World Unseen' will be a better movie when cut to three minutes and run in slow motion to a Beyonce song.

LISA

September 8th

I KNOW YOU'LL ALL forgive me not being terribly funny today. It's been a devastating time for us, since June, since finding out that Lisa has multiple myeloma. And if we felt bad, how much more has Lisa gone through... But what she learned and shared with us in June provided the ultimate test of how we, as human beings, react when thrown beneath the strongest pressure and when forced to face our biggest fears without flinching. And I am in awe, and inspired by, Lisa's reaction. Grace, elegance of spirit, clarity of vision. No complaining, no whining, no anger. Wow. I whine every day (as you all know!) about the silliest things. We all do. And it is something inherent in most human nature that, regretfully, we learn to appreciate and be grateful most when we are faced with the possibility of losing all we hold dear. Lisa was never like that, I have to say. She is someone with a rare zest for life, with a throaty laugh that you hear a lot when you're around her, someone who is introverted and thoughtful, but also appreciative of the little joys of life. What's truly admirable is that nothing in her attitude has changed. I know many of you feel upset and depressed by the news, because the movies have that rare and magical ability to transport you to a place you feel you know, and to put before you images of a face, a smile, and gestures that you learn to understand and predict, and which give you a feeling of knowing that person intimately. And I know you all appreciate the work she has done in all her movies, as well as 'The World Unseen' and 'I Can't Think Straight'. So I would say, acknowledge the sorrow, but let's give her the message that we visualise her in perfect health and starring in many more Enlightenment movies. There is a cure for everything that ails us - we just need to find it, or allow the body to find it. And if anyone has the mind and spirit to allow that healing to happen, it's Lisa.

Besides, I have two more scripts waiting, Lisa. And nice try, but you don't get off that easily...

Nurse Hanan taking Lisa Ray's temperature - at least, that's what she told me she was doing.

SHEETAL SPEAKS

September 10th

So HANAN ASKED OUR leading ladies what they thought of the new, incredibly sexy Box Set of 'I Can't Think Straight' and 'The World Unseen'. This is what Sheetal said:

'THE WORLD UNSEEN' and 'I CANT THINK STRAIGHT' together???? love it. Just got my box set and i am so excited that everyone is able to grab both of these movies that meant so much to us and we loved making! fabulous gift idea - treat yourself or a friend!! enjoy!'

So there. You love her and she loves it! Enough said. She is a woman of good taste, obviously. And the people of Dallas, Texas are equally tasteful, having just today announced Ms Sheth 'Best Actress in a Leading Role' at their festival for her performance in 'The World Unseen'. Now all of you Sheetal fans want to know how she is on set. Let me tell you. She's there early, she's always super-prepared, she eats carbohydrates as if preparing for a famine and she still has a flat stomach. And she gives me a hard time for being a Brit, and I might now and then accuse her of the worst stereotypes of her fellow countrymen. If ever there was the clashing of two cultures on set it happened between Sheetal (representing America in the red, white & blue corner) and me (representing the British Empire in the.. er..red, white and blue corner). So, apparently, for Sheetal it was laughable when the director of the movie ate her breakfast toast with a knife and fork. (In my defence, it takes proper implements to carve out the perfect mouthful of fried breakfast). And for me, I wept every time I shouted 'Cut', and Sheetal reverted to her American accent. But we reached a truce, where she just smirked while watching me eat, and I cringed only inwardly when she called Hanan 'HK'. (I hope you are getting the irony in all this, Mumbai journalists, who like to quote my blog - it's a joke!). I couldn't have had a better Leyla or Amina. Especially one that has the same initials as me. And as for the last question you all have - are those really her eyes? Well, I tried to get her contact lenses out, and I can tell you with complete authority that they are...

Shamim explains to Sheetal why Marmite, a black, bitter, British waste product of a brewing process, is the only thing to put on your toast in the morning. With a knife and fork.

THE WORLD UNSEEN
– TOTALLY SEEN

September 12th

SO SHEETAL CALLED HANAN last night, and they were talking about the love scenes in 'I Can't Think Straight'. How does that happen to come up in conversation, by the way? Never mind, I digress, as usual. Sheetal asked which 50% of the scene was cut in India.

'The part with you in it,' Hanan told her. Casting aside the producer's delicate and polite way of talking to the talent, I wondered if this might actually be a better way to censor half a scene - keep the whole thing, but just airbrush out one of the offending lesbians? That way, it would look like Lisa was just having a lie down after accidentally slamming herself against the bedroom door. I must call the Mumbai censor and ask. But later! I have NEWS!

Now, it is against every fibre of my being to use the word 'totally' in any sentence, but what I have to give you this fine Saturday evening is too cool, wicked, phat and otherwise, like, totally awesome to describe in anything other than my 'Sheetal' voice. Yes, you've seen 'The World Unseen' film. You've seen the behind-the-scenes on YouTube, and possibly the extended one on the DVD. You may even have bothered to listen to the gems of wisdom, wit and erudition that drop like pearls from my lips during the Director's Commentary. But you've never seen THESE interviews with Lisa Ray and Sheetal Sheth, or THIS footage from the set. Yes, all new, all brilliantly-edited together in one 6 minute orgy of orgasmic video footage....I give you, ladies and gentlemen (or is it gentleman - there's more than one guy on this fan page, no?!)...a brand new video EXCLUSIVELY on the Enlightenment Productions site, Media page. You won't find it on YouTube, or Metacafe or on the screens at Piccadilly Circus. It's only here. Enjoy. http://www.enlightenment-productions.com/index.php?page=media

'I can't believe they cut me out of the bedroom scene! I'm off down to the post office to see if that blonde postmistress is free for dinner.'

MUM'S THE WORD

September 13th

JUST BACK FROM SURREY, and a visit to my mother's with the boys. My aunt is here from Canada so it was great to see her too and another aunt I haven't seen in ages. I left Hanan at home to catch up with work. Or so she said. By the time we arrived, I was about ready to spit, because the combination of Luca asking 'Are we there yet?' every 10 seconds, and Ethan tormenting me with a 10 inch long rubber fly (yes like a disgusting house fly with eyes and wings and everything) had made me drive like a Formula One hopeful. As we screeched into the parking area, gravel flying, my sister (whom I had recruited for emotional support) confirmed that this hour trapped in a moving metal capsule with my offspring had been the best contraceptive she'd had in a while.

We rang the bell 17 times in 10 seconds (Ethan is very talented with reflexes) and we went in. It was like stepping onto the set of 'Lord of the Rings'. Over there in the Hobbit corner we had my mother and aunts, all 5 feet nothing of them. Over here we had my boys, long and beanpole-like and also nearly 5 feet tall despite being 10 and 6. It was very disconcerting overall, like being in a surreal soap opera for the vertically challenged. I darted around, feeling very tall, while my mother whipped out doughnuts and assorted goodies from the fridge and eyed me narrowly when I told Ethan to check the sell-by dates on anything that came out of his grandmother's fridge.

'Food lasts at least 4 days past the sell-by date,' my mother informed me with a hurt sniff.

'Yes but if it walks out by itself, it should go,' I returned.

In case you're wondering what my mother looks like, she had a cameo in 'The World Unseen', as the mother of the 'suitable boy' that is set up for dinner with Amina. She gave a bravura performance that totally justified every diva fit she had about hair and make up and frankly, I think if Sheetal had any decency, she'd give up the Best Actress awards and hand 'em over to a woman admittedly smaller in stature, but a giant amongst actors. Though, again, it was all in the direction. As we rolled the camera, I asked my mother to imagine how she felt when I first told her about Hanan. Or when she first ate a lemon. Either way, it worked. Anyway, I digress. We came, we ate, we eventually left and careered back to London. A long drive that I've made a thousand times, towards and away from Hanan, back in the old days. But it felt longer today, perhaps because of a wistful realisation that home may stay the same, but I haven't. Or maybe it just felt longer because I had a black rubber insect eyeing me from the back seat. Far better philosophers than I have pondered this dilemma. In the meantime, it turned out that Hanan had not only caught up on emails but had met a friend who'd invited her to the Berkeley Hotel for lunch.

'Really?' I asked, pleasantly. 'So while I was schlepping 50 miles with two over-active little people to meet Frodo for lunch, you were hanging out at the coolest hotel in Knightsbridge?' That's what I meant to say, but what came out was:

'How was that?' She grinned, cheekily. 'Oh, it was all right.'

The boys are suitably sorry that they tormented mummy with oversized rubber insects...

SHAMIM SARIF'S SIX DEGREES OF SEMI-SEPARATION

September 17th

Try saying that title very fast after a big glass of wine. I just did, and it's impossible. Or maybe it wasn't the wine that scrambled my brain but the three hours intense interaction with my adorable, argumentative children. When they are asleep they are so cute I could just eat them. And when they wake up, I am invariably sorry that I didn't. Anyway, I digress. What's new? Well, let me tell you. I received an email from a fan. Yes, one of the 1600 band of sisters and brothers who are bound together by ecstasy over 'The World Unseen', 'I Can't Think Straight', Leonie Casanova, or perhaps one of the thousand or so who just stumbled on me while looking for someone else beginning with Sh, like Shania Twain, Sherpa Tenzing or perhaps Sheetal Sheth. Anyway, this fan, Madison Le, who (like Sariena Carmichael) shall remain nameless lest I infringe on her privacy, told me she would like to donate items from the Enlightenment Productions catalogue (of incredibly high-quality yet reasonably priced products) as PRIZES. Yes. Another competition. I know what you're thinking. What on earth happened to the first competition? A long story, but I can shorten things as well as any Hong Kong tailor, so the story with the first competition, for the best fan video, is that we launched in a shower of sparks with a rather wonderful video (which you can see on this site) and then crashed in a ball of flame while waiting for our Indian IT people to actually sort out our site so we can receive entries. That will happen by tomorrow or Hanan will be on a plane to Delhi armed with her Palestinian methods of persuasion (including ropes and houmus).

In the meantime, Madison suggested another game of 'Six Degrees of Separation from Shamim'. Eg she met 'Jenny' from the L Word. Jenny knows Carmen. I know (barely) Sarah Shahi which = 2 degrees. This idea was scuppered straight off by my co-writer, neighbour and now ex-friend Kelly Moss who emailed a long list of immediate prizewinners, highlights including:

Kelly Moss... 'i stare at her every day, in fact i'm staring at her right now!'
Ethan & Luca Sarif-Kattan... 'we ignore her threats every day.'
grocery delivery man... 'I deliver 87 chickens to her every week.'
Hanan Kattan... 'I've slept with her!'

Added to the fact that half my family and a lot of fans I met at festivals are on this site, who all therefore have 0 degrees of separation, this isn't going to work. But Madison has another idea. Degrees of Shamim + 1. So to win, a fan must:

1. establish connection from me to them, however many degrees (photos welcome, I have nothing to fear having never been snapped mud wrestling or on the floor of a bar, at least not that I recall) AND THEN

2. establish a NEW connection, who has never heard of me, or seen/read my movies/books. The new connection must sign on as a new fan to this FB page and provide testimony to their introduction/interest to me and my work. And if, as I am sure all of you have, you've already bored your friends senseless talking about all things Enlightenment, then think of it as a chance to go out and find new friends!

One prize of a DVD will be awarded to the new connection and one prize of a T shirt to the fan. The first three pairs to both post are winners. And I'm going to let Madison judge. Instead of her donating the prizes, we'll donate them, and Madison will make the equivalent donation to Lisa Ray's chosen Myeloma fund. I think the Just Fans page should be where the connections should be posted. Confused? Don't be. Just let's see how it goes. Now y'all go forth and multiply.

Lisa Ray tries to figure out the competition rules without success.

KEEP THE LESBIANS

September 20th

So I FINISHED THE SCREENPLAY of 'Despite the Falling Snow' yesterday. I felt good about it, but handed it to my producer (aka the wife) with some trepidation as she has the diplomacy of Stalin when it comes to delivering her notes. I waited tensely. Problem number one - she is welded to her Macbook marketing 'The World Unseen' and 'I Can't Think Straight' until midnight every night now. I tried cajoling her into bed (to read). Nothing. I tried begging. Nada. Then I appeared with an armful of clothes and told her I was throwing them out of the window so that when I kicked her out, she wouldn't have to bother to pack. She glanced up at this. 'If you're making tea, can I have some?' was all she said.

I retired to the bedroom, defeated and feeling sorry for myself, but not so much that I didn't fall straight to sleep, on my back, so I would be sure to snore freely and enjoy my new-found single status. Around 12.30 am I was woken by the shifting of papers next to me and worse - the sound that strikes fear into the heart of the most confident writer - the scribble of pen marks vandalising my beautiful, perfect script. I lay awake seething and worried for at least a minute and a half before sleep overtook me.

Today I asked Hanan what she thought of the script. She loved it. But there was just one thing bothering her. The book of 'Despite' has a lesbian sub-plot and in my attempts to fit in all the intrigue, passion and betrayal of the main Russian story, I had cut it out. Now the producer wanted it back. I defended my decision, she stared me down without blinking.

'I need the lesbians in there,' she declared.

'You need them in there?! When did you turn into a studio boss with a cigar?' I asked, appalled.

'Are you saying I look like Harvey Weinstein?' Hanan responded.

Well, I don't care if I caught her having an orgy with 12 young women, I wouldn't ever accuse her of looking like Harvey (though obviously I might well spend time thinking up ways to make her sorry she was born). I resisted the urge to get high and mighty and listened, controlling the aggrieved artist's eyebrow that was dying to rise up sarcastically. And damn if she didn't have a great reason that helped the story along and made it all more plausible. The producer was right, and I would have been irritated except that I was excited to make the changes. She tried to get me to start right away but I resisted. For one thing, it's Sunday night. For another, I need to go collect someone's clothes from the ground outside...

'Gimme the lesbians, Sarif, or you'll be in the Venetian canal sleeping with the fishes. Kapish?'

SHAMIM SARIF

SEX IN SCANDINAVIA

September 23rd

So WE'RE OFF TO OSLO on Saturday for a screening of 'I Can't Think Straight'. Better than that, Hanan and I have been asked to do a panel entitled... 'Real Lesbians, Real Sex'. Well, bring on the schnapps. I instantly wondered what Fake Lesbians are and whether Fake Sex might be kind of like an erotic Tai Chi, where you move around your lover without touching them. But I digress. I have a list of topics to be covered, including what constitutes real lesbian sex, and whether it is accurately portrayed on film. Well. I panicked right there. 'You picked the wrong girl!' I wanted to email back, but how could I tell them that I haven't the foggiest idea what everyone else considers to be real, since I have only shagged (sorry, I meant to say, been 'romantically involved with') one woman? Luckily, that one (yes, Hanan! Who else?) is absolutely the best in the world when it comes to the topic under discussion in Oslo. How do I know this, if I haven't tried the 'world unseen', played the field, tasted from the smorgasbord of women out there? Because Hanan TOLD me so. And I have no reason to doubt her honesty on this point, do I? However, I considered my options in order to avoid showing up in Oslo unprepared for my fans (assuming there are any). Should I research? Gain more experience? I asked my wife, to see if maybe this would shock her enough to cast aside the laptop. She narrowed her eyes at the screen and said 'Don't let the door hit you on the way out. And don't come back'. I was only asking...

In other news, these are my last days in my thirties, as Hanan never tires of reminding me, ahead of my 40th birthday tomorrow. What better way to spend them than driving up and down London looking at schools to move our kids to. Just the application process for all that has driven me nuts. Lots of registrars asking if my husband will be accompanying me to see the school. My husband? Ah, no, but I'll bring my wife. Cue a delicate British cough followed by the thing us Brits do so well, which is to pretend we understood that all along. 'Lovely. Super. Fabulous.' Clearly none of these registrars have ever attended one of my Scandinavian Sex Panels. The deep joy of trawling around schools culminated on a freezing football field in Wandsworth, watching our younger boy in his first ever match. Any romantic ideal I had of actually watching him play was cast aside as Hanan thrust the zoom lens and camera at me. 'Get plenty of action shots,' she commanded. Have you ever tried to follow a herd of 6 year-olds up and down a pitch with a zoom lens? She sighed deeply and took back the camera, handing me the video instead. Our team lost 14-nil, and now it's all recorded for posterity. When we watched the playback, there was all this noise and shouting. 'Who is that obnoxious woman yelling at her kid to get the ball?' I asked, a moment before I realised it was me. Oops. Let's hope turning 40 gives me some maturity...

Fake lesbians about to have fake sex? Who knows? (well, I do, but I'll never tell).

SHAMIM SARIF

WALKING WITH LISA

September 25th

So I AM LOOKING AT 40 of the most perfect, beautiful, long-stemmed red roses as I write this, one of many gifts from my even more perfect, beautiful and perfectly-stemmed wife. It was a great birthday and for many reasons I grew up a lot more than I realised I would, and in a week or two I will be able to post another fabulous gift I received on this very page. In the meantime, let's move swiftly on to lunch with Hanan yesterday, and as she leaned across for the fifth time to pick something out of my hair or off my eyelash, we were reminded of Lisa Ray's obsessive preparation for 'I Can't Think Straight'. Even though Lisa knew Tala was a fictionalised character she spent every day of the two weeks before the shoot preparing for the role by observing Hanan with the unblinking stare of a sniper. Although she is obviously used to being stared at by beautiful women (and by me), Hanan still found this somewhat unnerving, and asked Lisa what she was doing.

'Sucking out your mojo,' Lisa would reply laconically, continuing to gaze on the producer. By Hanan's standards, this answer lacked a) clarity b) definition and c) bullet points and so only unnerved her more. By the time we started shooting, the artistic and languid Lisa had assumed so much of Hanan's inner workings that she was able to 1. multitask 2. speak in bullet points and 3. pick every piece of real and imaginary fluff off Sheetal. You may notice that several of these moments made it into 'I Can't Think Straight' - in the locker room after tennis for example. Anyway, I have a theory that Lisa's stalking Hanan on set was revenge for their first meeting, a year or so before, this time in pre-casting for 'The World Unseen'. Though ordinarily I am loathe to leave my wife in coffee shops with stunning actors, I managed to miss this meeting. Lisa showed up and they chatted for a minute or two, and then Hanan asked her what she thought of the script.

'I haven't read it,' Lisa replied.

'Have you read the book?' Hanan asked tersely.

'Nope.'

Hanan hailed a passing waiter. 'Bill please'.

But Lisa called her the next morning having stayed up all night to read the novel of 'The World Unseen', asked for another chance and the rest is history, and we will be championing Lisa as long as we can.

To which point, we know that Lisa is taking part in a 5 kilometer walk on 18th

October and is looking for sponsorship to support the hospital which is doing fantastic work in helping her conquer both the myeloma and her lingering need to pick fluff off her co-stars.

In the meantime, we'd like to announce that through our own Sarif-Kattan foundation (small, but hey, all oak trees were once acorns, and Pamela Anderson's boobs took a while to get where they are too) we will donate 15% of all sales of all products bought via the Enlightenment Productions site from today, 25th September until 31st October, to the same charity that Lisa is supporting. Books, T-shirts, soundtracks, DVDs, everything. So, if you were ever considering getting that 'I Can't Think Straight' T-shirt for your mother to see if she understood what it meant, or if you were thinking of giving your aging grandmother 'The World Unseen' with a note saying 'I'm more like Amina than you realised!' - now's the time! And please spread the word, so we can send Lisa a big cheque, and we'll let you know how much we raised when we're done. I considered going out and selling myself on the street, but seriously, is raising a dollar at a time efficient...?!

Lisa Ray, Hanan 'Tala' Kattan and Sheetal Sheth in a threesome on set.

THANKS FOR THE MOVIE!
CAN I HAVE YOUR WIFE?!

September 27th

So AN HOUR AFTER we landed in Oslo, we found ourselves in a Chinese restaurant (don't ask) eating dodgy chicken chop suey to a background of Chinese pop music inside (think Celine Dion with a ruptured appendix) and a lot of blond people passing by outside. The meal cost around seven thousand pounds, which I guess is why the only thing I heard about Oslo before we left was 'It's expensive. No, REALLY expensive.' An hour after that we were taken to an interview with a lovely man with 24 face piercings (I counted, while trying not to wince) and then to the Lesbian Sex panel, both of which were held on a big old cargo boat. I'm here to report that an hour of debate as to whether 'real lesbian sex' in films meant graphic happenings and hairy legs or soft lighting and sexy underwear left us all just as confused as when we'd started. I mean, has it really been a terrible chore for you all to watch Lisa in silk underwear and Sheetal with smooth legs in 'I Can't Think Straight' and 'The World Unseen'? Were you all secretly wishing for hairy armpits, Y-fronts and flourescent lighting? Anyway, no-one complained at the screening and we signed a lot of books and DVDs afterwards as all this month's screening sales also make the 15% sale price donation to Lisa Ray's fund. As I signed people's names, I realised that poor Norway is in dire need of importing more vowels (Ksjirty? How do you SAY that?!).

Next up was a lesbian bar for an 'I Can't Think Straight' party, thrown by the generous festival organizers, where the wine flowed and so did the women - to our table. Well, they were all so polite in the cinema, but give them a drink or three, and they're all over it. Or all over Hanan, to be precise. Here's how it went. I went to the bathroom, no-one talked to me. Hanan went and some cute blonde woman accosted her for 10 minutes. Back at the table, another young woman approached and told me how much she loved the movie, then asked Hanan to dance with her. Thank goodness Hanan turned her down, because it gave her time to be approached by yet another admirer who offered to explain to Hanan in detail how the tennis and polo scenes were all about sex and orgasms. I positioned myself next to a bowl of pickled herring, ready to launch a fish attack on the next person to make a pass at my wife and drained my glass of wine while I surveyed the scene. A cute blonde leaned in.

'I'm sorry I just took a drink from your glass by mistake,' she said. I wasn't thrilled, but wondered if this line passed as flirtation in Oslo.

'That's OK,' I said.

'No I really am sorry,' she clarified. 'I just had swine flu.'

I laughed so hard I nearly knocked over the herring. That Scandinavian humour!

'No, really I did,' she said. 'But I'm not contagious any more.'

I resisted the urge to leap across the bar and swill my mouth with the purest vodka I could find, as I pondered just one question. Why does Hanan get the offers, and I get the swine flu? Back at the hotel, where I was dousing my swiney lips in disinfectant while complaining about every woman that had hit on her, it took Hanan about an hour to convince me I was over reading things. My new sense of calm lasted all the way up to the airplane where we found our seats, across the aisle from each other. On my side, two burly blokes welcomed me. On hers? Two thin, sexy blondes. One was reading the FT, thus proving she was smart as well as stunning. And when Hanan got up to go to the bathroom mid-flight I swear they BOTH followed her. Incensed, I finally found a use for the stopwatch part of my watch. Hanan was back in 98 seconds. I was relieved. She's good at moving fast, but not THAT fast. But I'm not taking any chances – now we're home, I'm getting out the burqa.

Shamim Sarif & Hanan Kattan in front of the Oslo opera, in their last picture before Shamim was felled by swine flu and Hanan was kidnapped by a gang of Norwegian lesbians…

SAVING FACE

September 30th

So I JUST SPENT the last two hours on the top floor of Harrods, getting a facial, one of my many wonderful birthday presents from my Norwegian-lesbian-encrusted wife. I had dragged myself there after a morning of writing. Sadly instead of writing lesbians into 'Despite the Falling Snow', I ended up writing irate emails to journalists who thought Roman Polanski's arrest was outrageous. I worked myself into such an indignant fury that I got a headache and became convinced I was dying of swine flu. My head was raging, my skin felt hotter than tarmac in the desert, and only when Hanan took my temperature (without nurse's uniform or much patience) did I realise there was absolutely nothing wrong with me. Cheered by this, I presented myself at Harrods and was ushered to a purple velvet waiting room where I perched on a flamboyantly indigo velvet chaise feeling like Oscar Wilde, but without the witticisms or the boyfriend. I cast around for something to read. There was Vogue. Too many pictures. And more Vogues. More pictures. And Hello! Nothing but pictures. How puzzling. Do only illiterate women get facials, I wondered? Anyway, I was soon whisked into a room and examined by a beautician who asked me how old I was. I toyed with saying 73 just so she would tell me how great my skin looked but, having been on my moral high horse about lying film directors all morning, I hated to fib.

'I just turned 40,' I said.

'I would never have said you're 40,' she said, shocked. 'Only late 30's'

Since I was in my late 30s only a week ago, I didn't find this particularly reassuring. Never mind, she dimmed the lights and massaged my face with delicious smelling things for an hour and I forgave her and Harrods immediately.

In other news, who's joining us in Tampa? I know the Miami fans are already organising their carpool but I think more of you might consider coming over, since Sheetal just called us to say she's joining us for the screening (Friday 16th October). She asked me if I would wear a bikini in Florida. I wouldn't wear a bikini if I was the only surviving person after a nuclear holocaust. I'm not taut enough in the right places, frankly. Now, will she be wearing a bikini? I didn't ask, so make sure you come to Tampa for the right reasons! We'll also be signing DVDs, books and people's torsos (kidding about the books. I mean torsos) in aid of Lisa Ray's fund. So head to Florida for some sun and fun. I'll be the one in the floppy hat and sunglasses, protecting my 39-year-old-looking skin.

Sheetal catches sight of Shamim in a bikini

TWO WRITERS
ARE BETTER THAN ONE

October 4th

THERE'S ONLY ONE thing that makes Hanan happier than nagging me to write, and that's when she can nag two people at once. So it was that Lisa Ray, fresh from retreat in Vermont, found Hanan on the phone asking for 1. her next blog and 2. her new book. Which were the same things she's been asking me for. I took the phone in haste.

'Your wife is kicking my ass,' Lisa informed me. 'I love it.'

I was pleased to hear it, but assured her the joy of nagging would shortly wear off, leaving Lisa no choice but to get extensive facial surgery to disguise her appearance and enter a witness protection program to evade Hanan's enthusiastic badgering.

'What's your new book?' I asked her.

'What book?'

'The book Hanan says you're writing.'

'I have no idea,' Lisa replied. 'She just told me to write one.'

Look, that happened to me and now I have 'Despite the Falling Snow', 'The World Unseen' AND 'I Can't Think Straight' as published novels. So, although being hounded night and day by an excitable Palestinian is not quite the romantic vision I always had of pouring out my soul in a Parisian garret, I can testify that it certainly works.

And the rest of the weekend was fabulous. I had always looked forward to the day when we could take our children for lunch and maybe an art exhibition without diapers, tantrums or whinging (mostly from me, not from them) and that day arrived yesterday. After a Chinese meal (cheaper than Norway, but with the same Eastern Celine Dion howling her heart out over the bathroom speakers - do they only have the one singer in China?) we headed to the Royal Academy to see Anish Kapoor's exhibition. Well, he may have spent years of his life and enough money to buy three Chinese meals in Oslo on this exhibition, but for my kids it was just lots of strangely reflecting mirrors, and red powdery sculptures. My inner mommy alarm went off as the boys headed with glee to a room full of soft red wax that I am sure had taken Anish months to sculpt into perfect waves. Security guards tensed as the boys approached. Old ladies took cover. But yes, they still made it out with a finger full of red wax each. Resourceful to the end. I hope it stands them in good stead later in life, rather than landing them in prison. As we were about to leave, a very beautiful young Indian woman grasped my arm and walked along with me. I knew exactly what had happened - she was with her sister, and in the chaos assumed I was her - but for a brief moment, I felt what it must be like to be Hanan, to have stunning girls throwing themselves at you all the time. Then the young woman looked at me properly, screamed and ran away. That part doesn't happen to Hanan so much. But instead of smiling and moving on, Hanan tapped the embarrassed girl on the shoulder and told her she was PRIVILEGED to have held the arm of a super famous film director. I could see the girl looking at me again, thinking 'I thought Steven Spielberg was Jewish. And a man. With a beard…' But Hanan kept talking, and by the end of it the poor girl was mortified that she had been frightened off by a truly famous celebrity. I'm sure she's a fan of this blog as we speak. If you're reading this, gallery girl, you can head over to www.lisaraniray. com now and see if Hanan's persuasiveness has worked on Lisa…

Lisa Ray considers the topic of her new book while Shamim Sarif contemplates a new identity covered in red wax in the Writer's Protection Programme…

DRAMA, DRAMA, DRAMA

October 5th

HANAN HAS A VICE. Worse than a vice, actually, an addiction. High time I put it out there to you fans who think she's so pure. What is it, you cry? Drugs? No, she's high enough. Alcohol? She never touches it. Sex? She never touches it (ha ha, just a bitter joke from a writer made to write a blog at midnight instead of... never mind). No, her vice is DRAMA. The craziness, the wildness, the extreme emotions of life. The more the better, and if it doesn't show up, Hanan will find it. She's famous for it. So much so that on set, Lisa Ray's favourite thing to do was stalk my wife declaiming 'Drama, drama, drama!' in an Arabic accent.

Bear with me, there is a point to this. Anyone who has the 'I Can't Think Straight' soundtrack will know Natacha Atlas because we used two of her Arabic fusion songs in the movie - Ghanwa Bossanova and Kidda. So today, I took Hanan to see Natacha in concert. First up, the concert was in Islington (north London, we live south). Once we made it through passport control and immigration (just past Piccadilly Circus), Hanan was much happier and we parked right outside the venue, an amazing church, and cruised in to seats wherever we liked, and we liked the 3rd row, a mere spitting distance from Natacha Atlas.

Frankly, I knew nothing about Natacha and had no idea what to expect, except that voice, but when she walked out Hanan just about passed out with joy. In a word, the woman is a Diva, with a capital D. We're talking leopard-print dress slashed up to the waist, cleavage that makes Dolly Parton look like Shane in 'The L Word', and enough eyeliner to make Cleopatra wish she was bolder. She walked out, sat down on a red-cloth draped chair and broke everyone's heart with her voice. It was drama, romance, and more drama. Hanan was doubled over in a paroxysm of drama overdose. By the time La Atlas got up, right at the end, and belly-danced (I kid you not) Hanan had to be revived by paramedics.

My wife recovered enough to suggest that we go and 'say hello' to Natacha after the show.

'I wish we'd brought the movies for her to see that we used her songs,' I said.

'I already couriered them to her this afternoon,' Hanan said.

Of course she did. What was I thinking? So I mutely followed as Hanan marched up to the woman guarding the backstage area and asked if we could go in and thank Natacha. I don't know what it is about my wife that inspires either trust or immense fear, but the woman opened the door for us without missing a beat, and we were in, thrust into the (non-sagging) bosom of Natacha Atlas. She seemed so much more fragile and delicate in person. We chatted, she was lovely and had received the movies. And obviously, she wanted a picture with me and Hanan, so we kindly obliged...

Ms Atlas rests her weary head against my wife (what IS it with Hanan and other women) to take a break from the drama, drama, drama...

NO NIPPLES

October 11th

A BEAUTIFUL SUNDAY morning in the park with the boys, and my mind drifted to nipples. No, I do not make Polanski look like a Sunday school teacher. We were teaching Luca to ride his bike on his own, and as Hanan and I jogged alongside him like a couple of extras from 'Run, Fatboy, Run', we went past the spot where we shot the final scene of 'I Can't Think Straight' with Tala and Leyla on the bench. We'd had a very rough time the day before, shooting the first love scene. It had started, as so many days did during that shoot, late and stressed out thanks to the first (so-called) financier. With all the charm of an irritated Nazi, he called me in, waved Lisa Ray's contract at me and growled.

'This has a 'no nipple' clause,' he grunted.

This wasn't news to anyone. I like a nipple as much as the next woman, but I didn't need them in this movie. I kept quiet and waited.

'I want nipples. Go find Lisa and make her show them, or the shoot is off.'

I exited and found Hanan who was busy scaring Indian lighting crew into working faster. She saw the look on my face.

'What is it?' she asked.

'He wants nipples.'

She considered a moment. 'Do you want nipples?'

'Not really.'

Hanan rolled up her metaphorical sleeves and went to take on the So-Called, Unethical Movie guy (maybe I should shorten that to, SCUM, gosh that's an unfortunate acronym) while I went to see Lisa. She was waiting to start shooting, drinking herbal tea.

'What's the delay?' she asked.

'I've been told to convince you to give me nipples.'

Lisa sipped meditatively at her camomile. 'You want nipples, Shamim?'

I looked at her. 'It's terribly good of you to ask, but no. I don't want them.'

We sat there for a while, passing the time, and chatting till Hanan came down stairs.

'He wants Sheetal's nipples too.'

One thing I am is an equal opportunity employer. If I don't want Lisa's nipples, I don't want Sheetal's. All for one, and one for all. Suffice to say that Hanan's unique combination of persuasion and firepower enabled the shoot to continue and we enforced the closed set rule, meaning that only 7 crew were allowed in, and all of them women (except for Aseem, the DP, who despite having a face covered in hair and a propensity for calling Lisa 'Dude', is an honorary girl). Anyway, that's where my mind was as we let go of Luca and he flew down the road, riding on his own. I don't know where Hanan's mind was, but she was out of breath and had to sit down. I hope it was just from the bike ride...

'Is that a nipple, or are you just happy to see me?'

THE LION ROARS

October 15th

T WO NIGHTS AGO, we had Hanan's father over for dinner for his birthday. He is a lovely man with a deliciously dry sense of humour, and when you meet him, you can tell where Hanan and Ethan get their inability to sit still, and their need to do twelve things at once. It was a unique chance for me to observe the Kattan genes over three generations and frankly, once I accepted the mania and drama, it was entertaining to watch. In lieu of conversation, Hanan flipped open her Mac and her electric foot massager (I kid you not), and started Skyping Aida while relaying instructions to her sister from her father, and all the while Ethan was doing homework on his computer. But wait, I hear you ask. Who was making dinner, icing a homemade birthday cake, getting Luca ready for bed, helping Ethan with homework and pouring drinks? Why, that would be me! I whirled around like frenzied butler waving chocolate icing-encrusted spoons at a chocolate-encrusted Luca who was re- fusing to brush his teeth. Ethan looked up from his science homework:

'I need two rules for working safely with electricity,' he said.

I looked with mute desperation at Hanan. She didn't glance up from the computer but she felt the look and shrugged.

'Hire an electrician,' I told Ethan. 'And don't put your toaster in the bath.'

He started writing, freeing me to finish icing Luca and put the cake to bed. Anyway, a good time was had by all, especially when I got my hands on a bottle of wine, and yesterday was Aida's birthday, and we're only sorry we couldn't entice her to join us in Tampa so I could throw her into a crowd of cheering lesbians as her present…

Speaking of birthdays, when the boys first asked me what I'd like for mine, I told them anything they picked would be perfect, because I was sure they would consider the kinds of things Mummy liked.

'A remote-controlled car!' one shouted.

'SPIDERS!!' yelled the other.

Needless to say, I didn't hold out much hope. Luckily for me, the birthday fairy, other- wise known as The Diva Kattan stepped in and drove our under-age offspring to a liquor store where they picked out a breathtakingly expensive bottle of Bordeaux. It cost so much that I am still in the phase of just looking at the label while changing my mind daily over whether beef or lamb would work better with it (yes, I can really be scary to live with).

Now I ended up with much more than I deserved in phenomenal presents from my beautiful wife, and such thoughtful gifts from the friends that we had over for dinner that I can honestly say there was not one thing that I haven't used already, including the inflatable woman (that's a joke, my friends are far too tasteful for that). But prize for most unique gift went to Leonie Casanova (http://tinyurl.com/yjpnu7v). She arrived 'from a music lesson' (liar) carrying her guitar case like Julie Andrews in The Sound of Music (but minus the bad pinafore dress and page boy haircut obviously) and then stood up after we'd finished dinner and announced that her present was a new song that she would sing for us that evening.

Well, it was stunning, and captured all the emotion, intelligence and melodic brilliance that made Hanan and I jump on Leonie the first evening we encountered her genius in a smoky jazz bar. But then it was over. A fleeting moment of heaven, and now I wanted to hear it again. Luckily, our own personal CNN correspondent, Hanan Amanpour, had thought ahead and had lunged for the video camera as soon as Leonie started strumming. By the time she was done, we had it all on tape.

'We'll make a video for the fans!' Hanan announced.

'It has to be about Shamim's birthday, not the song,' Leonie said.

'No way, it's about the song, not my birthday,' I answered.

Hanan just shrugged and, like the mini United Nations that she is, managed to meld both our wishes together into one video. So, fans, super fans and mega fans, ladies, gentlemen and inflatable fans, I give you Leonie Casanova, singing 'I Wanted New York'. Enjoy

http://www.youtube.com/watch?v=z7stXfZtcxI

Leonie Casanova, from the same Russian village as Beyonce, sings about her favourite things.

FUN IN FLORIDA

October 17th

I LEAPT OUT of bed our first morning in Tampa, and threw back the curtains to let the Florida sunshine pour in. It was pitch dark outside. I checked the clock. 4.30 am.

'What time is it?' my wife mumbled.

'9.30,' I answered. I didn't add 'In London', but I crawled back to bed and fell asleep, leaving her to lie awake until the sounds of a tropical rainstorm outside roused me again. 'It'll clear,' I assured Hanan. 'This is the sunshine state'.

Well, we spent most of the day looking like entrants in a wet T-shirt contest but, luckily, the Tampa Theatre, one of the last remaining movie palaces in America, had it's own starry skied ceiling and truly stunning architecture. As we walked through the theatre to the green room, a woman began shrieking and tearing across the auditorium towards us. I looked behind me, expecting that Angelina Jolie was shadowing me, but no, the woman was heading for me and I knew it had to be a Facebook Super Fan, but all I had to go on are the little photos of all of you. She reached us at last.

'Sallie from Chicago,' she panted. 'You're all so much shorter than I imagined.'

Lovely to meet you too, I smiled, suddenly feeling like a Hobbit. Maybe I just have the stature of a giant in our You Tube videos, maybe I just looked smaller amongst the vast size of all things North American. Anyway, it was really wonderful to meet Sallie, as I do feel I almost know you all from your comments and photos. In the green room we all felt even tinier when we were introduced to Kathy De Buono ('Out at the Wedding') who is seven feet tall if she's an inch. I was beginning to get a complex, but there was no time to brood, because 'I Can't Think Straight' started and I didn't want to miss any of the story, because you know how hard it can be to catch up.

By the time we made it outside to the book signing, Hanan and Sheetal had fallen into their familiar pattern of bickering, a tradition which began on set. I signed a book and passed it on to Sheetal, whose leg generally taps up and down with compressed nervous energy.

'Here, sign this,' Sheetal said to Hanan.

'How about saying 'please'?' Hanan growled, thumping Sheetal's knee to make her leg stop jiggling.

'You wanna sign it or not, HK?' she asked, tapping the other foot.

'My name is Hanan.'

'Sure, HK.'

After an hour, I'd had enough and looked for help. Luckily, as I turned around, I found a policewoman standing right behind me.

'Can you sign this please?' she asked, waving 'The World Unseen' at me.

'Yes, I can but then I need you to handcuff these two together,' I said, cocking an eyebrow at Hanan and Sheetal.

'I'll chew off my own arm,' said Hanan.

Ah, the delicate relationship between producer and actor. Always a joy to watch. Luckily, the evening ended with more wine, courtesy of our hospitable festival progammer, Jill.

We're en route to DC now, having gone to the airport via the local public radio station for a live interview on the Woman's Show. My last radio experiences were at the BBC in London, which was all steel barriers, metal detectors, security badges and cubicle studios. Here it was like being in someone's living room – quilts on the walls, ornaments, a dog roaming around and hot coffee brewing. Even in the rain, I could get used to this. But Washington DC beckons followed by some time with Lisa Ray in Toronto, and so we have to leave the (alleged) sunshine of Florida for the cold cut and thrust of the seat of political power. Not that it bothers Hanan. 'I'm thinking to send Michelle a copy of the movies, and invite her to the screening tomorrow,' she just told me.

Michelle, Michelle, I pondered. Not a fan, I think. Is she a festival person? I rarely forget a name so I turned to her in chagrin. 'Who's Michelle?'

She regarded me with pity, as though I may have early Alzheimers. 'Michelle Obama.' She left out the 'Duh' on the end, but it was in her tone.

Right, then. I really hope she doesn't come, or I'm going to feel even shorter.

A friendly Tampa cop helps Shamim think straight by taking her into protective custody away from Hanan and Sheetal.

HANAN FOR THE WHITE HOUSE!

October 19th

Picture it. Saturday, late afternoon, Washington DC. Having spent a frustrating ten minutes suggesting to Hanan that you probably couldn't just courier a box set of 'I Can't Think Straight' and 'The World Unseen' to President Obama, I found myself in the back of a cab with Hanan, and an A4 envelope containing our movies. The driver asked us where we'd like to go.

'The White House,' Hanan informed him. 'Just to the entrance. We need to drop off a package.'

The cab driver regarded her in the mirror as if she had two heads. 'Lady, you can't just drive on up to the White House and say hey, here's a package.'

'No?' asked Hanan, taken aback.

'They got security and shit! I mean, what if that parcel's full of anthrax?'

She waved the box set at him. 'It's just DVDs. The envelope's open…'

He whipped around in his seat. 'And you know what else?' he cried. 'You look MIDDLE EASTERN!'

We got out of the cab and into bed, where we opened an email from Aida with the link to our live Tampa radio interview from earlier that day. Well, the interview was only 10 minutes long, but we were both fast asleep by the time it was done. I like to think it was because we were exhausted, not because we were boring. Anyway, here's the link, in case you feel like listening, just type 17th Oct in the Archive box, and we start about 6 minutes in.http://www.wmnf.org/programs/303

But I digress. Back to this morning, and we headed to the Corcoran Gallery to see a show by photographer Ed Burtynsky, whom we met through our dear friend and Exec Producer on The World Unseen, Katherine Priestley. It was phenomenal, but somewhat less phenomenal was traipsing around the park afterwards in a freezing gale to get a view of The White House. I watched Hanan nervously, half expecting her to whip a box set out of her bag and hurl it at the balcony, but we were much too far away, so she contented herself with stopping random tourists (always ones who spoke absolutely no English) to have them take endless pictures of us. And I contented myself with whining about the cold, until we found a cab.

As we drove past the sights, Hanan looked mistily out of the window.

'That's where my office used to be,' she told me. 'Overlooking that big white thing.'

'You mean the Washington Monument? And what do you mean "office"?'

'I had an office here. For a year and a half. Years ago'

Of course she did. I am married to Hanan, International Woman of Mystery. From Osaka to Shanghai, from Hong Kong to DC, from Paris, France to Waco, Texas -there's nowhere she hasn't spent time. I suppose it's a good thing that after nearly 14 years with her, I'm still finding out new things, but it does make me fear that if, during my ongoing application for Canadian citizenship, they decide to interview us to see if we're a genuine couple, we would both flunk unceremoniously. I told her this, and she assured me immigration would only ask about our favourite colours.

'What's your favourite colour?' I asked, realising I wasn't sure.

'Red,' Hanan replied without missing a beat.

'RED?' I was astounded. 'You don't wear red clothes, you threw out my only red shirt, there's nothing red in our house and you only wear black. What do you like about red?'

'I like the idea of it,' she said as if that ought to be obvious. I sat back and looked out of the window, pretending I was already being deported.

Luckily we were whisked away to the pre-screening brunch where more Facebook Super Fans (hello Jinnie, Madison, Lauren and more) were waiting. It's like a secret society now, everywhere we go, women pop up and know everything about us. Jinnie and Lauren took charge of the camera while Hanan and I met her friends, Rania (ex Chief of Staff for the King & Queen of Jordan) and Marwan (ex-Foreign Minister of Jordan and Ex Ambassador to Washington). I was becoming more and more nervous as to the Arab response to the political aspects of the film, but since they'd grown up with Hanan, they only wanted to discuss each detail of her five exes. This entailed talking through the entire film, so I was relieved when it was time for the Q&A and signing. From there it was straight to the airport, and you can guess that the reason for my second blog in two days is that I was trapped inside a sealed metal tube, in mid-air, sitting next to Hanan. I love that woman, but I love it more when we spend two hours laughing so hard we can't move, and less when she's cracking the whip. But hey, I'm not cold, so I can't complain. Sleep is for wimps. Blogs are for champions.

Hanan and Shamim shortly before being arrested for carrying dodgy DVDs to the White House and deported for not knowing anything about each other.

LISA RAY

October 21st

11 PM Sunday night, off a plane from DC and we're being driven through the quiet, genteel streets of Toronto to see Lisa. Haven't seen her since her diagnosis. We've seen her interviews, seen the pictures on her blog, but Hanan is still worried I will crack. 'Don't stare at her, if she doesn't look the same,' she tells me and I smile.

I don't know how to do anything else. I have spent most of two whole years staring at Lisa. Checking the light against her cheekbones through the viewfinder of a Panavision movie camera. Watching her in rehearsal, getting used to evaluating her on set, learning her mannerisms, noting the way her eyes reflect a genuine emotion found and rendered to make Miriam real in 'The World Unseen'. Understanding which moments are fall backs because she's tired, or because she temporarily has lost my view of the ephemeral essence of the scene after 12 hours of shooting and the 6th take. Gazing at the features she shares with Tala on a fifteen foot high studio screen, checking colours with clean, clinical concentration. Learning how to communicate with her to refine a performance, explaining without too many words – because, for someone who writes so well, she doesn't like too many words. The poet in her realised a while ago that words are a poor substitute for what we all yearn and love and desire, but that our humanity always makes us try and shuffle those words into patterns that evoke meaning. And feeling.

So we hug her and kiss her, and lie on the bed and touch hands, arms, whatever, all of us. It's a visceral need, to feel she is there and solid and with us when we were scared out of our wits by the word 'cancer', because there's a word that can evoke meaning for you, all of it layered with fear and sorrow. And I look at her, closely, for these two days, see the way the steroids have rounded her face, made her blowfish cheeks burn hot like she's holding coals in her mouth. And her eyes, liquid green and glowing. I watch her laugh and speak, dropping philosophy that stills us from her chapped lips with no effort, and I watch Hanan, my practical, beautiful doer and fixer, who cries silently as she holds Lisa because she can't fix her. Hanan, who always conceals the flayed, raw emotions of her heart under lists and bluster, but the cover is blown now, and that is hard to watch.

It's a lot to observe, a lot to absorb, and we spend every minute together, explaining, comparing, deciding but mostly laughing very hard. I cook, desperate to nourish her, marinating chicken, steaming rice, toasting pine nuts, crisping garlic, so much garlic, because garlic cleans the blood, doesn't it, it's better than a stem cell transfusion, better than chemo, better than anything else I can do.

So. How was it with Lisa? I can't tell you more than I've told you here – and it was a lot more fun than this blog. It was being with family, and the best kind of family. And I am sorry I did not make you laugh today, my lovely fans. I am sorry I did not make you drop your phone, or snort coffee through your nose, or wake your sleeping girlfriend with your giggles, or make you not care that your bike got stolen. You see, I remember the things you tell me, and I am glad for them. We'll laugh again in a couple of days, but in the meantime when you ask me how Lisa was, I can tell you that she was rightly once voted one of the most beautiful women of the millennium, and that it had very little to do with how she looks.

Hanan Kattan, Lisa Ray, and Shamim Sarif, the original 'Most Beautiful Woman of the Millennium' before losing her title due to overuse of garlic.

SPECIAL SERVICES
AND A HAPPY ENDING!

October 27th

So, AFTER A WHISTLE STOP North American tour during which I nearly succeeded in having Sheetal and Hanan arrested in Tampa, Hanan nearly got us both arrested sending DVDs to the White House, and I went underwear shopping with Lisa Ray in Toronto, we landed back in London for 24 hours before seeing what mayhem we could wreak on Portugal. But wait, I hear you cry. We heard about the Florida cop and the DC cab driver, but what's with Lisa Ray and the underwear? I know. After Toronto I gave you a heartfelt and meaningful encapsulation of the emotional landscape of our visit with Lisa, when what we all really wanted was to talk about bras and panties. OK, stop pleading, I'll tell you how it happened.

We were wandering up the road with Lisa to have lunch when she spied an Apple store.

'I want to get you something for your birthday, Shamimi,' she said, pulling me inside. I declined politely, I chained myself to trees in protest, but she was adamant.
'My present is being here with you,' I said. She regarded me with all the baleful suspicion that this reply deserved and continued to drag me around pointing out things I might like. As a Libran, I cannot commit to buying a newspaper without thinking about it for an hour or so, so I was quite distressed.

'I don't want to buy things I don't need,' I insisted.

'OK, then what do you need?'

The only thing I had come to North America determined to buy was underwear. It's easier, somehow, and cheaper, frankly. A gleam hit my eye.

'I need bras,' I said.

Hanan saw through my evil plan as if my mind was cellophane. 'You just want to be able to blog that Lisa Ray bought you underwear.'

Maybe I did. Is that such a bad thing? Wouldn't you brag about that? Exactly.

Cut to the next day. Lisa and Shamim occupy adjoining changing rooms while outside Hanan runs with a trolley through the aisles and sweeps large black T shirts into it by the armful. Now that I was faced with myself wearing nothing but a (very lovely) new bra and my old jeans, in a huge mirror with frighteningly bright lighting, my bravado was seeping away. Next door, Lisa tried on tops then whipped open my curtain.

'How're the bras?'

I sucked my stomach in and hastily put on my clothes. 'Perfect. I feel very uplifted.'

And so I did, and the uplifted feeling from my excellent birthday presents lasted all the way to the British Airways counter en route to Portugal. We checked in without incident (if you don't count the kids trying to check themselves in as luggage on the baggage belt) and as we turned away to leave the counter a young woman stepped up smartly and flashed her badge.

'Ms Kattan? Ms Sarif? Special Services. Step this way please.'

SPECIAL SERVICES?? STEP THIS WAY?? I've seen Hollywood spy movies, I'm a director for goodness sake! This was it. This was code. They'd discovered that I didn't know Hanan's favourite colour, that our life together was a sham, and we were being deported. That we had actually lived together for 13 years and were British citizens on British soil temporarily slipped my mind. All I knew was that we were headed to Guantanamo, and that orange jumpsuits didn't suit me, no matter how sexy my bra.

Elaine had by now introduced herself with great charm (my first inkling she might not be with the CIA) and we followed her to security where, with several crisp flashes of her badge, we sailed through. Of course, my Britishness meant I would rather be shipped to a hellhole than actually ask what was happening, but luckily I was travelling with Hanan, Interrogator Extraordinaire. She asked a few questions and Elaine told us her job was to help people who travel often with British Airways and also celebrities (with a nod to me) through the airport. Obviously I immediately thought that she had mistaken me for Angelina Jolie (stop laughing, I'll do the jokes) but it turned out she knew 'The World Unseen' and 'I Can't Think Straight', and was there to make sure the director and producer were looked after. Now I could relax about it, I took a moment to feel like a rock star and enjoy the attention. The boys eyed our escort uncertainly.

'Is she coming with us to Portugal?' the younger one asked.

Frankly, as we were led to the business class lounge, I thought that would not be a bad idea. Sadly Elaine had a lot more work to do and had to leave us there. But I want to thank her for making our day, and also allowing me to leave you with this gem of wisdom. You never know when you're going to be in a first class lounge, or strip-searched in a prison, but either way, it pays to have good underwear.

Lisa helps Shamim try on her new bra. At least, I think that's me…

SHAMIM SARIF

I FORGOT WHAT I REMEMBERED TO TELL YOU

October 31st

So IT IS GOODBYE to Portugal, where Hanan's favourite aunt has looked after us so well, it was like having BA special services with us after all. The intriguing thing about my Palestinian wife is that she seems to have cousins, aunts and uncles in every corner of the world, but one of the best things about her aunt is that she talks to me only in Arabic, even when we're alone, even though she speaks perfect English, and even though my Arabic is limited to two handy phrases - 'Can I have a felafel with extra garlic please?' and 'I don't belong in Guantanamo, but do you have a blue jumpsuit anyway?' Anyway, thanks to her amazing generosity, our time here has been a wonderful mixture of great food, massages and traditional fado (Portuguese songs of yearning), but not all at the same time.

On the final day, after a morning's work, we shepherded the boys into the car for a last run around the beach. Hanan had not fully disengaged from work mode so she was driving the way she works – furiously and without noticing that she didn't own the road. Unsurprisingly, we overshot the turn off to the beach as we thundered down the tarmac road like Thelma and Louise. I hung onto the hand strap and screamed as Hanan wrenched the car into a turn. The boys blanched and nearly threw up as the stench of burned rubber poured through the open windows. Hanan, wearing shades and an oblivious attitude, cranked Leonie Casanova's 'I Wanted New York' louder on the CD to drown out my weeping. It was like a scene from the Bourne Identity. Nauseating, scary but super cool.

On the other hand, all my attempts at coolness come to nothing, and I suspect that is because coolness cannot be bought, learned or faked. Like a sense of rhythm (something that also escapes me), you've either got it or you ain't. But I realized I had crossed the bounds of nerdyness into something more worrying when I got out of the shower, where I had been attempting to wash the smell of scorched tyres out of my hair. I dried off, picked up a bottle of something that looked familiar, and slathered it over myself. Only when I was fully coated in a layer of soapy slime did I realize I had attempted to moisturize with shower gel. I got back in the shower, and recalled another incident the day before that had also made me fear for my sanity. I thought of the movie 'Iris' and felt hard done by for I hadn't imagined losing my marbles until I was at the Judi Dench stage, and here I was, barely past Kate Winslet. I called to Hanan in such a tormented whine that she immediately abandoned her Macbook and strode to the bathroom.

I told her what I had done with the shower gel. She bit into an apple and said nothing, which was just as well, because I wasn't finished. Eyes misting over as I slipped into a satisfying, treacle pool of self-pity, I begged her to put me in a home at the first sign of dementia, to just lock the door, toss the key into her cleavage and get on with her life without so much as a backward glance. I wouldn't want to hold her back from finding happiness with someone else, I continued, and she should always remember me as I once was, a witty, brilliant writer, unable to dance but willing to try...Practically sobbing, I watched as she continued chewing her apple impassively.

'Who directed 'I Can't Think Straight'?' she asked.

Clearly she was testing my memory and sanity. I bridled at the attempt. 'Martin Scorsese,' I sniffed, irritated.

'Who wrote 'The World Unseen'?'

'Jackie Collins.'

'Who buys your bras?' she grinned. Well, there was no way I was going to lie about that one.

'Lisa Ray,' I admitted.

'I have news,' Hanan grinned. 'You're not senile. You've been like this since we met.'

Hmm. I watched her leave the bathroom as I replaced self-pity with self-doubt. What did this mean? Would she lock me up? Would she throw away the key and cavort around the world picking up lesbians at festivals…? Clearly not, because she just reminded me that we have around 30 hours in London before we turn around to attend the TED conference in India. Then she told me the 30 hours included a lunch with friends for Luca's birthday, trick or treating with the kids, going to the office, cooking dinner for her dad, unpacking and re-packing. So why India? Well that was Hanan's 40th birthday present to me, and how it came about is a story in itself, but I'll keep that for the next blog. If I can remember to write it.

Hanan kisses Shamim goodbye before pointing her in the direction of the Atlantic and assuring her it's the way home.

INSANITY IN INCREDIBLE INDIA

November 5th

WE HADN'T HEARD from Lisa Ray for a few days, and when she didn't respond to Hanan's insistent messages, it was time for me to send a one line email from India.

'Are you on the roof?'

'No,' came the response. 'I guess I'm in the basement, since everything's upside down here.'

'Where?'

'South America.'

As you can tell, Lisa and I often email as if we're telegraphing each other in 1929 and every word costs a fortune which irritates Hanan as it leaves her without the detail she likes. What she had gleaned is that Lisa had decided to fly down to Buenos Aires when Dr Kattan had instructed her not to, and that meant that Hanan was now on the roof, and not in a good way. To calm her down I bundled her onto a TED bus to visit a Tibetan Buddhist monastery outside Mysore. What could be more calming than a long drive towards 700 chanting men in robes, right? Well, the first person we met on the bus was a charming woman. She asked where Hanan was from.

'I'm Palestinian,' Hanan replied.

'Really?' she responded, excited. 'I'm Israeli!'

I considered throwing us both out of the window before another Middle East conflagration engulfed us all, but our new friend was charming and open-minded, and she and Hanan spent the three hour round trip banging out a new peace process. We took a well-earned break to see men in saffron dresses, and we took photos with the monks and then got our karmic payback when an enormous family of Indians crowded around us to take a photo with me and Hanan. We were in quite a rural area and I somehow doubted they were 'I Can't Think Straight' fans. Actually, I think they just wanted to take a picture with the weird-looking Indian girl.

Back at TED, Hanan was noticing that we were sharing a campus (Infosys) with 10,000 young Indians, 5000 of them good-looking young Indian women, who all looked better in a shalwaar kameez than me. She also revelled in the lunches and dinners, all with plenty of Indian food (although, I suppose in India, it's just 'food') and asked me why, when I loved cooking, I couldn't cook much Indian food. I was sensing a theme here, a delicate comparison for her Indian-heritaged wife to the true Indian women here, and I wasn't coming out well...Luckily, we were taken off the Infosys campus for dinner, which made everyone happy, as the campus is very beautiful but very dry, and I don't mean it lacks rainfall. A long-awaited glass of wine in the lush garden of a beautifully lit palace hotel, while the South Indian rain poured down was a stunning sight. And the people we met were quite something. From the man who invented a needle that self-destructs after one use (saving 300,000 Indian kids from death by infection every year), to His Holiness the 17th Karmapa (a young 2nd in command to the Dalai Lama, who Hanan marched up to and shook hands with, to his glee and to the consternation of his Tibetan entourage), to an indomitable Indian grandmother in a sari who belts out Gershwin standards like Ethel Merman - it's an extraordinary mix of people who are all passionate about what they do. As everyone was roused to clap along and dance I realised that, apart from lacking the ability to wear a sari, and cook a good daal, I was also possibly the only person of Indian descent who has no sense of rhythm whatsoever. By contrast, I was married to the only Arab woman who could do a decent impression of Aishwarya Rai tossing her hair and dancing around to Bollywood beats. Seriously. I am jet-lagged, surrounded by non-Indians dancing to Bollywood choreography, meeting monks, Swamis, and tech geniuses, listening to the most intense lectures, eating four plates of daal a day on an alcohol-free campus and Lisa is in the basement in South America. If this is how it feels to be sober, will someone please send me a bottle of Bordeaux?!

Shamim introduces her wife to her extended and hitherto unknown family in a Buddhist temple in Mysore…

BOMBAY DREAMS

November 13th

I think it was when I jumped on stage to dance to Bollywood numbers with the 100 other people led by the Slumdog Millionaire choreographer, that I realised I was infected with India. Nothing could stop me, not even Hanan's aghast look as I moved my arms the opposite way to everyone else. No, for a brief, glittering moment, lit by spotlights, some colonial palace behind me, I was Aishwarya Rai - at least on the inside. I thought that, after that, the final hours of TED could do nothing more to complete my Indian odyssey, but more was to come when we had breakfast with Eve Ensler (the genius behind The Vagina Monologues and V-Day) and lunch next to His Holiness the Karmapa. Yes, it was a blast, AND we got to eat daal every meal, which combines deliciousness with colonic irrigation.

And so on to Mumbai, for a big meeting, and I stayed with Aseem, my brilliant cinematographer from 'I Can't Think Straight', and the man who worked so hard on 'The World Unseen' in post production. He and his wife Leena are the most enlightened, kind and funny people I ever met. They sort of drift around telling the best stories which alternate between profound Indian mythology and deeply hilarious behind the scenes snapshots of Indian film sets, and in between they do the work of ten people. I hated to leave them, but I needed to go home to Hanan and the boys, and besides I'd had enough of musing about why everyone, even women in saris, keep spitting on the pavements, or why car horns are used as a communication tool every two seconds. And I am sorry I didn't get to meet the Mumbai fans. I had forgotten how it is to make plans in a city where a) people call to set up a meeting as they are on their way to see you b) the traffic makes Piccadilly Circus feel like a bike trail. Plus my first encounter with Indian Chinese food did me in more than any wine-fuelled dancing could have. And so, I came away from India having met one fan at least, Kusuma in Bangalore who greeted us with beautiful flowers and breathlessness. I'm sure that happens to Aishwarya a lot.

And so back to London where I looked forward to peace, quiet and a gentle welcome home for the weary traveler. Of course, during this reverie in the car home, I had temporarily forgotten whom I was married to. And so, I dropped my bags at home and rushed to Luca's class assembly, where he had a lead role, and then after helping him and 15 other hyper seven year olds change back into uniform, I collapsed into the car and begged to go home to a hot shower and sleep.

'You're not coming to the office?' Hanan asked.

'I've been on a plane all night, haven't slept in days and I don't feel well,' I whined, as we pulled up outside the supermarket. Hanan thrust a list into my hand.

'Here. We have 10 people for dinner tonight.'

I knew that, of course, and it was for such a dear friend that shopping and making a home made birthday cake was a pleasure (I skipped the office!) As I staggered into bed at midnight, I looked forward to an easier day to come.

'We're moving offices tomorrow,' Hanan reminded me. '4th floor. No lift.' Why did she have to say it out loud? I mustered just enough strength to start weeping. And so, I am behind on the blogs. But, you'll be happy to know that Hanan has been nagging me non-stop since I landed to post one. And I feel she's recruited spies onto her side. I just fell asleep with the boys while allegedly putting THEM to bed, and I woke up to find them staring at me...here's the blog. I'm off to sleep. I hope.

Shamim shows off her moves shortly before being arrested for disturbing the peace.

FISHY BUSINESS

November 17th

AND SO, we are back in autumn in England, and the gilt-edged invitations are hitting the doormat. Before you get excited (or start laughing) at the idea of me hoisting on tights and a black dress, let me say that these are mostly invitations for our boys to interview at schools. I have no doubt that having tea with the Queen requires less formality. Applying to new schools has been such a test of endurance and nerves that I actually set up a whole spreadsheet to make sense of it, an act of insane efficiency that sent Hanan wild with excitement. And so, with interviews approaching for two boys whose preferred mode of communication appears to be silent telepathy, I sat down with Luca over breakfast to slyly conduct a test interview. As he spat toast crumbs everywhere I started with an easy one.

'What's your favourite subject?'

He chewed impassively. 'I dunno'

'OK. If you had to choose a subject, which one would you pick?' I responded, pleased with my savvy interviewing skills.

'What's a subject?'

I went off to get my own toast.

Back at the office, we are newly installed on the fourth floor (no lift) which means that after staggering up the stairs every morning, I can wait for my ears to pop and entertain myself by watching a series of student interns half my age panting their way in. By the time Hanan arrives, she has had plenty of thinking time on the stairs to come up with a whole new marketing strategy daily and a new To Do list for me. It's only a matter of time before she installs an oxygen tank to deal with the altitude, and enlists a Sherpa to carry her Macbook.

And so to the Finnish Embassy for a film party this evening. When we first got the invitation we weren't sure if it we were being set up for a practical joke. I mean, Finnish films aren't that well known (hence the party I guess) and you name a famous Finn movie (except Finding Nemo). But we rocked up to Kensington Palace Gardens, which is very lovely and high security, and there was indeed an embassy and a party. The other invitees were companies like Disney and Xbox. Yes, it was them, and us, the makers of blockbusters 'I Can't Think Straight' and 'The World Unseen'. We got some brilliant advice on online marketing, so good in fact that Hanan dragged me away from the array of pickled and smoked fish and bundled me into the car so we could get home and make notes. Or blogs. But I'm going to see if I can get a tea break now. Chomping herring is thirsty work and I need to excuse myself from the vicinity before my wife realises I've been making up keywords with the word Finn in them…

On the coast of Portugal, Hanan waits for Shamim to swim back from Finland with a bikini full of herring.

GIVE PEACE A CHANCE. ESPECIALLY FOR YOUR WIFE

November 23rd

So I WOKE UP in the morning to find myself face to face with an eyeball and it didn't belong to Hanan. Don't get ahead of yourselves, this is not a confession of anything dodgy. This slimy, bloodshot eyeball was not attached to a person, it was just stuck to the side of my bed staring at me like a producer willing me to finish a script…yes, the boys never fail to go to bed without thinking of beautiful things to leave for the mothers who have endured countless sleepless nights for them. I'll stop now, before the violins kick in.

The day got better when Hanan announced that she wanted my script and shot list.

'Script for what?'

'Our new Middle Eastern cooking show. We're shooting it in two weeks.'

When I finished crying, I asked her more details. She's been planning this for a good while, to be fair, but since I was appealing to you all for help finding a presenter just a couple of weeks ago, I didn't take it seriously. When will I learn? Nothing stops La Kattan, and sure enough, about ten seconds after I landed from Mumbai, she had set up a meeting with a very old friend who looks incredibly young, who loves food and cooks it, and who is half Lebanese, half Syrian and married to a Palestinian. If that woman can't figure out what to do with a dead lamb and some rice, no-one can. As ever, my pared down bumbling idea that a couple of us might just show up with a DVCam and give it a shot was blasted out of the window and I found myself in a full scale production meeting about prime lenses, 3rd Assistant Directors and Production Designers. Ahh, it felt like prepping for 'The World Unseen'. It even felt like prepping for 'I Can't Think Straight' (but without the harassment and weeping). So now I am behind a script, a shot list and a concept, but in the name of research I am retiring to bed (relatively) early and watching 'Caramel', a beautiful film set in Beirut. If you haven't seen it, please do.

In other news, Hanan has been busy embarking on preparation for the TEDx conference that she decided to host with the lovely Israeli woman we met in India. The idea is to bring together Palestinians and Israelis, with a focus on women, who are doing interesting and remarkable things in a world where it is hard to focus on anything but survival. Hanan is from Jordan, but before that she is from Jerusalem and Bethlehem which feels very meaningful to someone born in Surrey. The event is almost a year away and it's already been quite an effort in diplomacy which, I suspect, is the one subject Hanan must have flunked in school. So we've had protests that only Palestine should have a TEDx conference, we've had hassles about the name. Hanan's wonderful cousin Muna from Bethlehem even sent us Palestinian football kit for the boys. It had to be a place, and we didn't want an Israeli name or a Palestinian one, but something inclusive. Some incredibly brilliant genius (I can't say who, but she was struggling with shot lists for kebabs at the same time) came up with 'Tedx HolyLand'. What do I think? Funny you should ask, because I was just about to tell you. I think that anything that humanizes two opposing camps to each other can't be a bad thing. I think dialogue might expose pain, it might get nowhere, but it might, just might, get someone somewhere to think differently. And I think, like any good Brit, that sitting down over a nice cup of tea and a biscuit, even in the Holy Land, is definitely the way to go. 29th October 2010, East Jerusalem. Be there or be square...

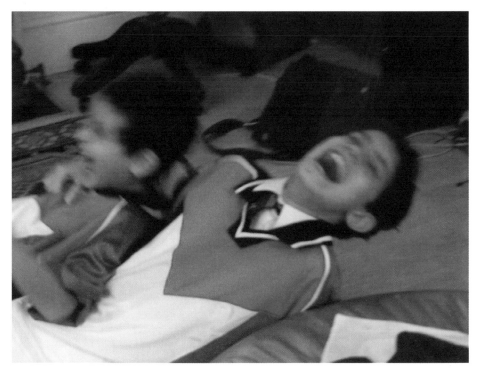

The boys are filled with remorse about the eyeball incident...

143

MERDE!

November 26th

I KNOW I AM formally in production for a shoot, when my kind, caring wife leaves her body and a head-spinning demonic producer person takes over. This person does not care whether I am tired, hungry or overworked, she just wants everything ready and NOW. So I rushed to work, tried to answer 120 emails in 6 minutes and then found myself in the nearby café having an interview. Piece of cake, I told myself. A chat about 'The World Unseen' and finding your path, about comedy and taboos in 'I Can't Think Straight'. I sipped my coffee and waited for the journalist to ask the question. 35 minutes later I was still waiting as he wanted to explain his theory on both films as the opening to my answer. It seemed like an excellent theory but he kept using words like pedagogical, oedipal and dialectic and you know, a cup of coffee will only get you through about 10 minutes of that. When he finished he looked at me expectantly. Hanan who had been fidgeting next to me for a while, looked at me expectantly. As casually as I could, I wiped the drool from my mouth and wondered if I dared ask what the question was again? Anyway, I got through it, realizing that Amina was indeed an oedipal rebuttal of the patriarchal symbol of dialectical learning and pedagogical craven backpedalling educative reductionism. Poor woman, no wonder she always had her hands in her pockets.

From there it was straight over to North London (Hanan packed her passport) to watch Mireille, our Middle East cooking show presenter, whip up a couple of recipes. This went well and gave Producer Hanan (as opposed to Wife Hanan) plenty to focus on other than me. As Mireille fried onions, Hanan emailed interns, made shopping lists, instructed her on camera technique, made calls and had me take photos and footage. On the way back, the Evening Standard called to ask for an article on Civil Partnerships.

"OK but I'm on a recce for a shoot. When do you need it?'

'4pm'

I looked at my watch. It was 3.30pm. I looked at Hanan, watching for any signs of weakness.

'No problem,' I said.

After that, despite tending to a child with temperature on the one hand, and another child with homework meant for someone aged 17, Hanan hounded me for my cooking show script and shot list. Her Producer technique is just to keep asking 'Do you have the script yet?' and unless I put it in her hands, she ignores my increasingly hysterical answers and threats of divorce, and keeps repeating it. I can weep, shout and grumble, nothing moves Producer Hanan.

'You don't love me.'

'Of course I do. Where's the script.'

'I'm going to leave you.'

'Does that mean the script's finished?'

So I finally sat down to write the script yesterday morning, sick child in bed, the other one whining about an essay on corporal punishment when Hanan told me we had to go to the park to shoot a video. In French. Listen, I love Paris as much as the next person, but I know enough to order steak frites and a nice Bordeaux and that's it. Whereas Hanan, whether in Wife or Producer mode, can speak French as if she was born beneath the Eiffel Tower. Which I don't rule out as a possibility until I've seen her original birth certificate. When we got back, we had to shoot another video for the new Enlightenment Productions website, launching in January. This one was in English, but by the time Hanan finished picking fluff off my hair, dusting my clothes and coaching me to be less wild but more funny, all I could say was 'Merde.' Funny that. A bientot.

Shamim (holding another birthday present from her missing wife) before shooting herself writing a pedagogical script for a cooking show, in French

CIAO, ITALIA!

December 5th

I LEFT FOR Florence with a deep sense of unease. Lisa Ray's dad called me, poring over the recipe I emailed for the Fatet Djaj (chicken, rice and houmus) that I had cooked for her. He couldn't find the Middle Eastern spice mix we left for him.

'Can I use garam masala instead?'

'NOOO!' I screamed, but luckily, only in my head.

'Maybe' I replied politely.

'And I have a lot of limes,' Mr Ray threw in. 'I was going to use them instead of lemons'. My inner Nigella wept. This wasn't Palestinian chicken any more, it was chicken vindaloo in a fajita. I am the kind of person who panics when I can't time a boiled egg with a stopwatch, and no-one can make me breakfast because I am so anal about the toast being hot and the tea being drinking temperature all at the same time. So this news about limes and masala weighed heavily on me until Hanan asked me politely to get a grip. There was no time to waste because we were boarding a flight to Florence.

You know that T shirt – 'Italians Do It Better'? Ok, it is a bit 1980s, which is when half of you were born, but then the Vatican is more on top of popular culture than I am. Anyway, it's true, about Italians. OK, perhaps they're not better at organisation particularly, or timings, as Hanan found when we got to the fabulous old theatre and she cornered a random festival person by backing them against a coffee machine.

'When is our movie playing?' she asked.

'Midnight. Or maybe 10.15?'

'Is that for sure?' Hanan asked through gritted teeth.

'Probably. We're not sure.'

But you know, timing isn't everything. I considered this as I inhaled my third plate of pasta while regarding Italian people skimming past the window, the men gorgeous and full of attitude, the women gorgeous and full of style. While I was just gorging and full of food.

My sister happened to be in Italy at the same time and so came to the 'I Can't Think Straight' screening with her boyfriend. I was afraid it would be him, her and 300 lesbians, but there was a high percentage of men, quite unusual during gay and lesbian festivals, and great to see. The response was ecstatic and the Q&A was in Italian! The long-lashed Fabrizio, organiser of the festival, made a fantastic translator, transforming even my most clumsy replies into a cascade of sexy Italian philosophy. And, as has lately become tradition, I met a FB fan, and she looked just like her photo, which is always reassuring. The lovely Sabrina drove from Rome to see both films, a trip of 300km which we so much appreciated.

Back home, Luca is fully recovered from swine flu just in time to play an Icicle in the school Christmas play. It's funny how you can find a child in white tights, tinsel and a ton of make up cute, as long as it's your child, but that all too brief moment was not enough to sustain Hanan through another hour of three-year old dancing reindeers, so she started scribbling me a (new) To-Do List and coming up with new and brilliant ideas to fill my spare time over Christmas. On the other hand, I am determined to feel the spirit of Christmas (and I don't mean lots of alcohol) so we took the boys to buy a tree this morning. The smell of the pines, the rustle of leaves, it was all fabulous. Not so fabulous is decorating the tree. It's an annual, subtle battle between the parents (one colour baubles, delicate lights, tasteful) and the kids (As many clashing colours as possible and enough flashing lights to cause an epileptic fit). I'll let you know who won next time. For now, I have to go and pick the tinsel out of my hair.

And one final thing – Hanan just spoke to Lisa to let her know that Enlightenment Productions raised $5000 for myeloma research from the percentage of sales from the end of September to November. You've all been amazing in ordering, re-ordering and spreading the word. Lisa is touched beyond words, and so are we. What can I say, except 'grazie mille' to the best fans in the world.

Surrounded by gorgeous Italian women, Shamim keeps a firm hold on Hanan under the pretence of being affectionate.

SHAMIM SARIF

LET HER EAT CAKE!

December 13th

Two women fall in love, against all odds. Gender, religion, race – none of these stars align. But there's another factor throwing them into dis-alignment, a deeper mismatching that didn't make it into the fictional world of 'I Can't Think Straight'. And it's sandwiches. Yes, you read that right. While I can't walk past a coffee shop without drooling at the idea of a cheese and pickle sandwich, Hanan views two slices of bread enclosing anything, especially when slathered with mayo or worse, mustard, as the lowest form of human expression. I was reminded of this when we found ourselves in a Pret between meetings with no option but a sandwich for sustenance. Excited, I skipped along the refrigerated sections, spoilt for choice. Horrified, Hanan desperately seized a felafel sandwich, a choice which could only go badly for someone raised on hot, homemade felafel in Jordan. We ate. I smiled. She whimpered.

'There has to be a sandwich you LIKE,' I said, not without a modicum of irritation.

'Yes. I had a fabulous sandwich once,' Hanan replied.

I brightened. 'You see! Where?'

'The Four Seasons George V in Paris. Remember that club sandwich?"

I cast my mind back, and recalled the fleetingly delicate taste of freshly seared free range chicken, encased in organic lettuce plucked but an hour beforehand, and wrapped in homemade bread finely sliced by some blonde and buxom sous chef, spread with butter salted from the dried tears of virginal maidens.

'I remember it cost 42 euros,' I said.

Hanan raised an eyebrow and I was saved only by a stranger who stepped up and asked if we were the makers of 'I Can't Think Straight' and 'The World Unseen'. Yes, added to my unique achievements of having written novels, raised two boys under eleven who can make a three course meal from scratch, danced on a Bollywood stage (albeit to the beat of a different drum), I can now say I was recognised in a coffee shop. I tried to be cool.

'Yes, I'm the director of those movies,' I said nonchalantly, wiping mayo off the side of my mouth. The woman peered at me, uncertain.

'I wasn't sure about you,' she said. 'But I recognised her,' she continued, beaming at Hanan.

Of course you do, I thought. If I met someone who would only eat a 42 euro sandwich, I'd recognise her too.

And so on to the cooking show. 'Middle Eastern Flavours' got underway in earnest after a few false starts when our glamorous presenter had a small panic attack under the gaze of the camera, lights and mini-feature film sized crew that Hanan had assembled. A shot of brandy helped her no end (yes, it was 10 am but we told her it was definitely cocktail hour somewhere in the world) and we were on our way. It was frenetic, frightening and fun. All the adrenaline of being on a shoot coursed back into my veins as we tried to make breasts look more attractive (chicken breasts, obviously) and there was not a sandwich in sight nor, sadly, a buxom sous chef, though I asked Hanan to help chop more than once.

Hanan came down with a high temperature after the two day shoot and couldn't get up by late afternoon Saturday. The stress of getting everything organised over the past several

148

months, for this and a ton of other projects, kicked in, and she was subdued all weekend, emerging from the duvet at regular intervals only to ask me if I'd finished my blog (apparently she was ill, but not that ill). Still it was the quietest weekend I'd had in years, as I happily told Lisa Ray when we called her.

'Is Hanan sick?' she asked with uncanny precision. We discussed Argentinian book stores and racist dogs for a while, the kind of conversation that makes Hanan want to weep, before she wrested the phone from my hands and talked to Lisa about assets, business opportunities and time lines.

I ended up in the cinema with the boys, watching Planet 51, the point of which I am still not sure of, except to give exhausted parents time to sleep amongst wriggling toddlers and the stench of old sweets. I passed the (endless) time by watching my children fill their faces with stale popcorn. By the time we staggered home at 7pm in the pitch dark, they couldn't face dinner.

'What did you give them to eat?' Hanan grilled me, as if I was a cheap cheese sandwich.

'A little popcorn,' I admitted, defensively.

'It was HUGE,' said the little one, who hasn't learned the art of limiting information, holding out his arms to indicate the bucket of rubbish I had paid almost 42 euros to feed him with.

Hanan regarded me narrowly as their Omega 3-rich fish and rice and broccoli went untouched.

'I'll just go and write my blog,' I said and disappeared as fast as I could.

On their wedding day, Shamim renounces any food slapped between slices of bread and promises Hanan she will only eat cake, a promise she would break within 24 hours...

149

CHRISTMAS SPIRIT

December 18th

A TINGE OF SNOW in the air, the smell of decaying Christmas trees and the shrieks of children filled with chocolate Santas and hyperactivity - I knew it was time for my annual lunch with Kelly Moss. Since Kelly is my co-writer on 'I Can't Think Straight' and one of the Executive Producers, and since I am the other writer and the director, we feel justified in referring to this 3 hour long homage to red meat and red wine as the 'office Christmas lunch'. Anyway, it's become an annual tradition, and one of the few things (along with runs in the park, grocery shopping, cooking and kids' homework) that Hanan generally steers clear of. Today, however, as she dropped me off outside a pub sporting fairy lights without and a fireplace within, she waved folornly.

'I'll just go home and have some salad,' she said.

I hesitated. It was zero degrees. A random snowflake grazed Hanan's head.

'Why don't you join us?' I offered. She considered. I knew she was drawn by the idea of warmth and hot food, but balked at the idea of sitting with two people who find themselves much more amusing than anyone else seems to.

'Would you like me to join you?' she asked.

Now that's a loaded question.

If you've ever been married to a woman - no, actually, if you've ever had a relationship with a woman, slept with a woman, or just spoken to one in a bar - you will know that there is only one correct answer to that question.

'Of course I do,' I said. And, in fact, I did. I love having my wife with me everywhere. But, where Kelly and I tend to sit about for hours admiring each others ability to make limericks out of the word 'dissolute', Hanan tends to order her main course and the bill at the same time and expect intelligent conversation in between. The 'office Christmas lunch' has certain standards, all of them quite low. Could two diverse cultures meet? Thinking of Tala and Leyla, even Amina and Miriam, I knew they could. So, I breezed into the dining room feeling goodwill to all women and we sat down with Kelly. I greeted her. Hanan greeted a passing waiter:

'We need to be out in an hour and a half,' she said. Hmm. It was downhill from there. We ordered the steaks and wine, but it wasn't the same with Hanan watching my glass ('You have to work') and picking stray bits out of my hair while silently miming to me to sit up straighter. Call me a grinch, but by the time she had admonished the waiter for taking three whole minutes to bring coffee, while Kelly and I galloped through a shared dessert trying not to chew so many times, I was filled with a warm Christmas feeling that was more like heartburn than compassion.

We hit the pavement towards the office leaving Kelly still draining the dregs of her wine, and as I hurried after Hanan tripping on my half-worn coat, she turned and watched me. I thought I felt it all. The irritation that she'd wasted all this time on two people who weren't funny enough to write a cracker joke, never mind a movie. The horror that she was married to someone daft enough to trip on her own coat. But her face broke into a smile.

'That was the most relaxing meal I've had in ages,' she said. I smiled too, relieved.

'In fact,' she said. 'I think I'll join you every year!'

Marriage. The agony and the ecstasy.

Hanan is banished to Siberia following her dissolute behaviour at the Office Christmas Lunch...

HAVE A HAIRY HOLIDAY!

December 20th

So LISA RAY goes into hospital tomorrow for the stem cell transplant. Long phone calls between her and Hanan, filled with vision and practicality in equal measure, and shorter bursts between Lisa and me discussing our future life eating steak and reading books in Argentina, which I think Lisa fell in love with on her recent trip. I wanted her to try Hanan's stem cells, mix them with her own, just to see what a driven, over-achieving actor with curlier hair looked like. But she has plenty of her own so she needs no bodily parts from Hanan or anyone else. In fact, with typical generosity of spirit, she's sending us a Fedex.

'Don't send anything,' Hanan commanded.

'What is it?' I said, excited. 'Chocolates? Christmas cake?'

'Hair,' said Lisa.

That shut me up. 'Hair?' I pondered. 'Whose?'

'Mine.'

Yes, anyone can send a cake for Christmas. Not everyone couriers their own personal shag pile. Apparently, she has a big bag of her recently shaved hair hanging around. She's been tweeting about it. No wonder she has 10 times the number of followers I have. We discussed the hair for a while. It will be strange to see it without Lisa underneath it, but more than that we have to decide what to do with it. We reckon that, since she has several months of non-working recovery still to come, we should use it to raise money towards Lisa's medical costs.

Since I never really left behind my love affair with Keats, the Brontes and all those true Romantics, my first thought was to come up with a necklace and locket, inside which a lock of Lisa's hair would be curled.

'Brilliant idea,' said Hanan as I gave myself a mental gold star. 'Lisa's fans could buy it for their girlfriends or boyfriends for Valentine's Day.'

I don't know about you, but if my wife confronted me on Valentine's with a piece of jewelry containing the hair of a stunningly gorgeous actress, I might start crying. And not in a good way. But then I thought she had a point, because I have a ton of emails from people who thought 'I Can't Think Straight' and 'The World Unseen' were the most romantic movies ever, so a lock of hair from Tala/Miriam's head might be just the thing. And what else can you do with a mane of a goddess? Knit a scarf? Make high-end dental floss? Sell sticky facial tufts so you can recreate Robert Pattinson in Twilight in the comfort of your own home?

Lisa has a week of intense chemotherapy coming up, during which she will lose more hair (I asked her not to sweep that into a Fedex bag) followed by a couple of weeks in isolation while her immunity is at zero. Then it's a few months at home for recovery. So let's come up with some hairy ideas to warm her up in January.

In the meantime, Lisa has sent a message to everyone, and asked us to post it. Here goes:

To all Fellow Yellow Diarists, Enlightened Friends and Supporters-

There has been such a constant outpouring of love and generosity since I began the Yellow Diaries. As I prepare for the final leg of my treatment for Multiple Myeloma, a lot of you have asked how you can continue to support this journey.

First know that I am grateful for all your open hearted responses already.

Second: please do not illegally download the films into which Shamim, Hanan, Sheetal and I have poured our creative energies. Purchase 'The World Unseen' and 'I Can't Think Straight' from the Enlightenment website and you will be supporting not just the films we created, but future film projects made with passion and integrity. Without this support, there will be no more. In addition, we the artists collectively cannot sustain ourselves financially if you are watching the fruit of our labour for free. Think about it- its difficult enough to remain true to your vision and passion. Working with Shamim and Hanan has been deeply inspiring and I would like to work with them again and again. I would like to continue to make my living as a actor committed to working on projects which illuminate and provoke. This can only happen if you express your support by buying the films.

Happy Holidays and a Yellow Wish for all-

Love,

Lisa

Lisa and Hanan in Vancouver, back when Lisa had hair, Hanan had an hour off and Shamim had to stay home and look after the kids.

CLUMSY...BUT SHARP

December 27th

CHRISTMAS COMES but once a year, and Hanan is one person who remains grateful for that. My wife was staggering around the living room at 7am gathering used wrapping paper, as the boys played with their presents. Bent double, clearing up after the kids at the crack of dawn is bad enough, but it also meant she didn't notice Ethan's new remote controlled helicopter heading straight for her curls. There may be more stomach-churning things to watch than whirring blades whipping through extremely curly hair, but I can't think of one right now.

'My head!' Hanan cried.

'My helicopter!' yelled Ethan.

'My scalpel,' I called.

It took me a solid five minutes of unravelling to get the helicopter blades separated from the curls, after which Hanan was in need of Christmas spirit more than I was, except she doesn't drink. That didn't stop me cracking open a bottle before I attacked the chicken carving with gusto. Just the week before, I had received a late birthday present from my sister Anouchka in the form of a knife skills class. I had visions of placing Hanan against a wall and stunning our friends with a display of blade throwing that left every hair on her head untouched and ready for altercations with flying toys. But the class was all about cooking - my second favourite subject (after eating). Suffice it to say that we prepared and enjoyed a three course meal that was positively crammed with chopped, cut and sliced ingredients, but my favourite part was jointing a chicken. Yes, my days of reaching over, grabbing a leg or a breast and pulling are over, at least when it comes to roast fowl. Feeling quite superior about my general kitchen abilities, I got a bit blase with the knife by the time we got to slicing mangoes, and I sliced into my finger instead. As much as this was shocking to me, it was quite conceivable to my lovely wife, who explained to me that while I have a vision of myself in my own mind as something of a female James Bond (panther-like reflexes) the reality is that I am closer to Mr Bean.

Feeling a little aggrieved, I asked her to prove that assertion (even though the first and last time we did an aerobics class together 13 years ago in Thailand remains a mortal stain of shame on my lack of rhythm).

'On the set of 'I Can't Think Straight" she replied. 'I hired a runner just to follow you with a fire blanket and a first aid kit.'

'That was three years ago,' I said defensively. But Hanan was ready with the more recent example of the shoot of 'Middle Eastern Flavours', the new cooking show.

'I can't believe I would suggest you direct anything that involved naked flames and sharp knives,' she said, clearly still upset with her own lack of judgement.

'I didn't notice anything fall, or break,' I returned.

'Because I was behind you, catching everything,' Hanan said.

And that's the thing, you see. She has that Bond-ness in her. She can drive up a mountain, listen to educational CDs, make To Do lists and admire the scenery all at the same time and still cling to hairpin bends like white on rice. I know she probably did sense a falling light from the side of her eye and whip out a hand to catch it while I bounded over to the production designer, oblivious. Perhaps that's why I got one of the best Christmas presents ever, in the shape of a leather backpack that can hold everything I own in one go (so I don't forget my phone, keys or computer each day). But I can't avoid the fact that I just found one of her presents in the back of the cupboard because I forgot I'd bought it. But you know what I decided? I may tap dance (or fall down) to the beat of a different drum, but no-one knows how to handle a (chicken) breast like me...

Shamim sharpens her knife skills, learning how to skewer anyone who doesn't find her funny.

Behind the Scenes on *I Can't Think Straight*

This was the picture Leyla pulls off her noticeboard in the movie — we took it in the park before shooting began.

156

People don't usually think of how the set looks. There's a lot going on that the actors have to ignore.

157

There was more than one relationship between women in the film… Nina Wadia and Antonia Frering getting on better off camera than on.

With Lisa Ray, laughing through the constant problems that came up during the shoot of I Can't Think Straight.

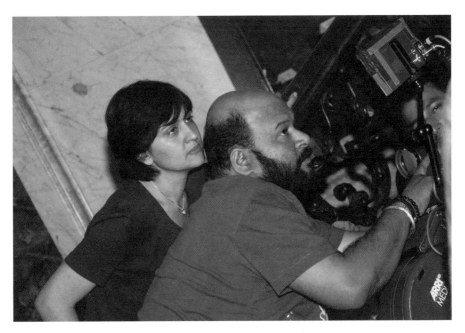

My amazing, supportive and genius cinematographer, Aseem Bajaj. Always showing me things I couldn't see, cinematically and spiritually.

A quiet moment on set for Lisa Ray.

Producer Hanan Kattan prepares for her cameo as the Jordan lecturer.

Behind the Scenes on *The World Unseen*

Lisa and Sheetal on an impromptu shoot in the beautiful landscape behind 'Miriam's Farm'

Lisa waits for a shot on set. A huge amount going on around her.

*Producer Hanan Kattan, Line Producer Carol Prentice and Co-Producer Brigid Olen
hard at work on logistics on set.*

The sound department gets close.

Our sons Ethan and Luca prepare for their scenes in the make-up van.
Lisa Ray behind them.

The kids get their own 'trailer'…

The director tries out the crane.

Hanan, Shamim, Brigid and script supervisor Kim around the monitor. Usually when directing I ask Hanan to watch the monitor while I stay behind camera near the actors, but this was a crane shot and I needed to make sure the camera movement worked well.

Are Sheetal's eyes really like that?! Yes, they are. Enjoy.

*Ethan examines the camera while waiting for a shot. We used a Panavision and shot on 35mm film –
something outside the budget, but Hanan managed it by using a camera and lighting crew from India.*

Lisa's portrait from a deleted scene where she prepares the spare bedroom for Amina to stay the night.

Katherine Priestley, our dear friend and one of our incredibly supportive Executive Producers came to visit us on set.

And Hanan's sister Aida quit her job in LA to come and work with us on the film. This was typical of the passion shown by so many crew and cast.

There was passion on set too…

The kitchen scene was the last scene we shot. We wrapped the production, then found out there was a scratch on all the negative from that day's shoot. We had to regroup and shoot the whole thing again. Despite that, or because of it, we laughed a lot during that scene.

Sheetal waits for a shot…

As do Hanan and Parvin Dabas (Omar)

*That driving lesson looks so intimate in the film – but less so in reality with
assorted crew and lights all around.*

Parvin has fun on set during a night shoot.

Going over the script – Lisa's hair protected with the blue cap.

178

Sheetal and Leonie on their café set. We shot the interior in a real café in the Woodstock area of Cape Town. Tanya van Tonder worked wonders with production design.

Sometimes there's just too much to juggle. Directing a baby proves hard work.

179

Ethan and Sheetal get into a bubble-blowing competition to while away the hours on set.

Leonie, Hanan, Shamim and Sheetal hang out at the café.

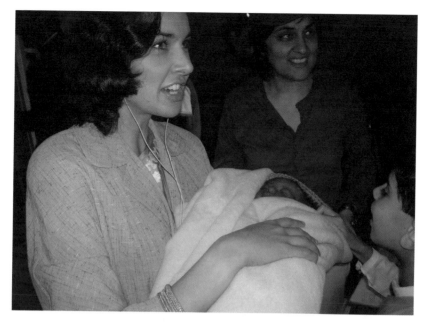

Lisa with her 'baby' on set.

The producer having a good day on set

Checking a shot with cinematographer Mike Downie.
Mike was the third Director of Photography we had on The World Unseen!

The parties before the shoot! From left, Colin's girlfriend, Desi (publicity), Colin ('De Witt'), Anouchka (my sister), Tanya (Production Design), Sheetal ('Amina'), Shamim, Shaz (our housemate), Rod ('Sergeant Stewart'), Katherine (Exec Producer), Parvin ('Omar') and Brigid (co-producer).

Lisa doesn't need much help to look fabulous, but gets a little assistance anyway.

Lisa and Sheetal stay in character between shots.

Behind the Scenes on *Broken* and *Little Feeling*

*Leonie Casanova sings against a projection of Lisa Ray in
'The World Unseen' for the video of 'Broken'*

Hanan and Leonie watch playback on a shot from the 'Little Feeling' video, shot in Berkshire at the home of our good friend Antoinette Claessens where we also shot parts of 'I Can't Think Straight'.

187

Leonie warms up Lisa Tchenguiz, one of the Executive Producers of 'I Can't Think Straight'.

A Note from Hanan:

(Note from Shamim: This really is what Hanan considers to be 'brief')

It is hard to know where to start as there are so many memories from making both films that they could fill books and volumes. Since my lovely wife thinks I like to communicate with bullet points, I shall try to keep this brief and focus a bit more on the production process instead of the behind the scenes stories which I will leave for my wife to unravel (or not).

I am not sure if any of you know what a Film Producer does? Many of you have asked. Here is a flavour for those who are not familiar with what it entails to remove any illusion of glamour and to give you a small taster of what it takes. Needless to say, multi-tasking and organisation are paramount in most things and especially when producing.

'Pre' Pre-Production:

We start with a script that is locked. Shamim likes me to get involved with her creative process from the first draft stage whether it is for her novels, scripts, music or poems. Next is the creation of a business plan and then approaching potential investors for funding. This part can take years, but I'll fast forward...

Phase 1 - Pre-production:

Once the funding is secured then there are hundreds of contracts to be completed with investors, cast, crew, locations and the list is long. During pre-production, which is the period before the shoot, it becomes like a military operation, at least as far as I am concerned, as everything needs to be 100% in place for when Shamim is ready to call 'Action.'

We then do the casting, Shamim assembles her creative team while I assemble my production team and the 'drama, drama, drama' begins. We do the location recce to find the most suitable locations for each scene and then we negotiate and hire the locations. Shamim briefs her creative team on her vision for the look and feel of the scenes, the characters, the colours and palates of the film and the feel she is after, the way the hair and make up should progress based on each character's arc and the same for each character's wardrobe and how the wardrobe may progress to match the arc and growth of each character and so on. It all has to match the feel and mood and progression of the story, the characters and how they interact, what they wear, how they look based on how they feel and how they evolve. It is intricate and fascinating to observe as it unfolds and all the department heads have their teams working for them and we have weekly meetings between the production team and the creative team to make sure everything is moving smoothly towards one goal; the shoot...

Phase 2 - Production:

During pre-production, my production team is busy with every detail of the shoot from making sure we will have catering and food to feed everyone, to arranging portable toilets near the locations, hiring the lighting, camera, sound and all equipment needed for the shoot as well as hiring the creative and productions heads and teams, arranging the cast movement and travel arrangements and visas, obtaining production insurance, getting the key cast, director and myself to have medical check ups which are needed for the insurance and the million and one things that are needed to ensure a smooth shoot from start to end.

Nothing can go wrong during the shoot days (that is the aim) and massive planning takes place throughout pre-production to make sure everyone knows where they need to be each day, what equipment is needed, which shots are taking place and so on. We allocate funds for each department and I have to sign cheques each week and I have my budget review meetings weekly with our film accountants and my production team to make sure that we are on budget and to deal with any issues or problems that are arising as we progress towards the shoot and as issues occur to handle them calmly and of course to report to the investors on progress and that we are on budget and on time.

Then it is rehearsals with the cast, hair and make up trials, fittings for their wardrobes, entertaining the cast and looking after them.

The hours are very long when we are shooting and I am on set daily with Shamim but I stay near the video monitor while Shamim is with the actors on set. Some producers come on set only occasionally but I find it important to be there as an extra pair of eyes for Shamim and to make sure the set is running smoothly and to deal with any issues that might pop up while shooting. There are always issues to deal with on set and I like to make sure I am there daily to sort out any issues that might occur.

There's always an incredible energy on set and it is non-stop. Shamim likes to be on set early with her cast when they are having their hair and make up done to make sure all is in place and she blocks her actors, goes over her shot lists with her key team for each shot which is a crucial process to get the shots needed for each scene. That often means Shamim has to leave at 5 am to be on set in time as we normally start shooting early and everyone has to be fed, in costume ready with hair and make up, rehearsed and the lighting and the set design all in place.

When we wrap each day, the negative goes to the lab for processing and we get daily reports on the condition of the negative as well as other technical reports and Shamim and I go to watch the rushes late at night with the editor who is working away on the processed film each day. After many long hours on set, and driving to locations and back which could be over an hour each way, it is tough to go see the rushes in a dark room with the editor when all we want to do is to be in bed in a dark room. And this brutal schedule continues for 6 days a week non-stop (on I Can't Think Straight we did 14 days shoot in a row before having one day off and then back again for long stretches).

Shooting an independent low budget film is brutal as the hours are long and the time is tight to get all the shots that are needed each day especially when shooting on 35mm film as we did for both films. And the weather has to be on our side as well as the sun and the wind to avoid delays and to ensure continuity.

After the wrap party and when everyone has gone home, we are fully in the edit suite and I am there with Shamim daily to give my input as we progress and the production team needs a couple of weeks to wrap up after the shoot itself is wrapped. The shooting is usually the shortest phase of filmmaking.

Phase 3 - Post Production:

Here it is all about editing, music composing, recording, mixing, colour correction, opening and closing credit titles, deliverables - the list is long. This phase is often the longest phase of filmmaking as it is quite technical and artistic in a very different sense.

The challenge for us due to budget was to organise post-production in different continents and countries. We did the editing of both films in South Africa and part of the post-production in Cape Town where we lived for 10 months with our boys to prepare and to shoot 'The World Unseen'. It was wonderful for us to move as a couple and a family to a new continent and a new country and for the boys to be intimately involved in their mommies lives throughout while adjusting to studying at a relaxed South African school after the very strict British school system they were used to.

We returned back to London, settled the boys in their old school and then we did the majority of the post-production (grading and pre-mixing) in Mumbai (thanks to Aseem Bajaj, our amazing cinematographer who made this a possibility) which meant many long trips for Shamim to Mumbai and I would join her for stretches at a time as one of us had to be there for the boys. Juggling work (with crazy hours) and a family is not always an easy formula but with military-like planning, we made sure it worked. We did the final sound mix at Pinewood studios in the UK as well as the final prints in the UK. The film negatives flew to South Africa, then India then the UK for the final mix.

We lost the original sound to a crooked first investor, and despite winning the long court case battle in London, he would not release the original sound so we had to re-create the sound from scratch (every breath, every move, every sound) and of course the cast had to do the ADR (dubbing) with all their lines. This unfortunately meant that we can never have 100% perfect sync in 'I Can't Think Straight' and the cost to do the sound entirely from scratch was another big budget that needed to be raised.

Considering the journey of this film and that 'I Can't Think Straight' risked never seeing the light of day, we decided to live with a film that had some parts of it out of sync than not having a film at all and thankfully as fans love our films, they are forgiving of the sync issues in I Can't Think Straight. Our fans seem to have developed a cult like following of both films and have been beyond amazing and supportive of us and our films. So thank you everyone for the massive and continued support which is very much appreciated and crucial for independent filmmakers.

The music score of The World Unseen was recorded live at Pinewood with amazing classical musicians from the UK who were hand-picked by our talented score composer Richard Blackford for The World Unseen. We recorded some of the score and the song 'Hey Girl' for I Can't Think Straight with Raiomond Mirza, our amazing score composer, in Mumbai. The rest of the songs we recorded in London with our amazing and talented Leonie Casanova who has become a very dear friend and family to us.

So it was a fusion of music, colours, cultures, continents, food and cast to get those films made and with a lot of love, tenderness and passion. This could not have happened without the belief in us and in the material from our Executive Producers who invested in both our films and made our dreams into a reality and without the support of our cast and crew who believed in us and who went out of their way to make it happen.

Final Phase - Going to Market

Once the films are locked, it is about taking them to market to sell them to distributors and to release at major film festivals where distributors come looking for new films to buy. But this is another dissertation.

I see my role as a Producer is to be focused on bringing Shamim's creative talent to the screen giving her as much creative freedom as possible within the constraints and limitations of working with small to medium budgets and to bring her vision and the end result to as many people as possible. And if I am going to dedicate so much time and energy on producing films, I will do so for Shamim's work as I am passionate about her work and vision which reflects our outlook on life.

As for stories from behind the scenes of both 'The World Unseen' and 'I Can't Think Straight', there are many funny moments, some sad moments and some hairy moments and maybe one day Shamim will write a book about it and some stories will just have to stay in the dark.

Why Do It?

Having read the above (and I only kept it brief) you might think why do it?

I found out soon enough one must be a little mad to get into the film business and passion for the material is paramount. The rewards of seeing the work come to life are immeasurable and beyond gratifying. Supporting my brilliant and creative wife while enjoying the process of creation (despite the pain I give her) is breath-taking. Meeting wonderfully creative people along the way like Aseem, Leonie, Lisa and Sheetal and the other cast and crew as a result of both films has been inspiring and I have learnt from each one of them.

Despite the bumpy start with our lovely Lisa Ray when we first met in London when she did not realise you don't show up to a meeting without reading a script, in fairness to Lisa she came around quickly and amazingly and with complete pro-fessionalism and thankfully she did as Lisa added many layers of richness into our lives and we are blessed to have her as a life long friend and as someone who is closer to us than family. Lisa continues to teach me so much about life and living and I look forward to a continued warm and loving friendship for many, many years to come.

And I look forward to many decades of creativity and brilliance with my lovely wife through films, books, music and all the wonderful things in life that elevate the mind and spirit and make each day a most fulfilling adventure that is even richer by sharing it with my loved ones and with fans and people who are touched, moved and inspired by the work. What a wonderful journey it has been and here is to many more amazing years.

Acclaim for
The World Unseen Novel

"It is an impressive debut. Sarif's story brings together the descriptive power of the novelist with the screenwriter's mastery of dialogue." *The Times*

"I read The World Unseen at a gulp, so entrancing is it's style, so complete it's tale of love and betrayal, and so accurate it's depiction of the physical, social and political scene..." *Johannesburg Star – Book of the Week*

"Sarif's elegant and understated debut eschews emotional fireworks, and offers an unusual insight into early apartheid . . . a novel that lives up to its title" *The Times - Play*

"In the tradition of Vikram Seth, Sarif throws down a literary gauntlet that very few writers will be able to pick and return with any conviction." *Pride*

"A really wonderful book. Sarif's writing is delicate and confident and the characters are real and very believable." *Maggie O'Farrell, Author*

"Highly original... this is a stylishly written work. Sarif is near faultless..." *India Weekly*

"The characters shine with the beauty of Sarif's deceptively skilful prose which keeps your eyes skating along the narrative in sheer enjoyment. I read this book in two long sittings, unable to put it down." *Dyverse*

"If you only read one novel for the rest of the year, make it this one. Sarif is a new writer who deserves to win prizes." *Waterstones*

Acclaim for
Despite The Falling Snow

"Despite the Falling Snow by Shamim Sarif, one of our most outstanding young novelists, is my novel of the year: its delicate artistry and immense compass reaches back to the labyrinthine heart of Soviet Russia.' *Stevie Davies, The Independent*

'Sarif's thrilling new novel makes me think of the 'The English Patient' and 'The French Lieutenant's Woman'. Like those books, it has at its core an unforgettable love story. Yet Sarif also understands the human cost exacted by totalitarian systems. And she knows that the worst betrayals are those committed by the ones we love. Her novel is immensely powerful – and deeply moving.' *Steve Yarbrough, author of The Oxygen Man*

'A perfectly balanced novel of love and tragedy…brutally shocking. The beauty of the streets of Moscow, the bejewelled architecture of the metro stations, is all a majestic backdrop to a play of mistrust and deception, where friends, even the best of friends, can turn against each other in fear.' *Waterstones Magazine*

'This story is, quite literally, breathtaking.' *The Good Book Guide*

'Explores love and tragic loss with the pace of a thriller and a style that is gentle and flowing, a hypnotic combination that eases between the US and 1950s Moscow… A pure delight, highly recommended.' *The Bookseller*

'An intriguing story of love, betrayal, anguish and despair . . . Shamim Sarif brings her characters to life with a delicacy of touch evocative of the intensity of their passions. An enthralling read.' *Daily Dispatch*

'A compelling read, flicking expertly between the tragic present and tumultuous past…Haunting at times, Shamim's elegant prose weaves a poignant tale indeed.' *Crush Books*

'Shamim Sarif's intense and elegant first novel drew on her South African roots. This one shows that her cultural compass can stretch even wider without dulling the delicacy of her gaze….Highly readable.' *The Independent*

Acclaim for
I Can't Think Straight

'…a brilliantly executed, romantic, sexy, and heart-warming page-turner… I Can't Think Straight is a novel that all readers and all critics, regardless of sexuality, would agree is the work of an amazingly talented writer and one that is a refreshing and immensely enjoyable read that leaves you smiling. The only thing to not like about the book is that it had to end…' *Cherrygrrl.com*

'Each character in the story is wonderfully complex and endearing… Sarif evokes an atmosphere so diverse and inviting, each page is something to be savored. Sarif's descriptions are beautifully crafted; delicate, seductive and enthralling, they make I Can't Think Straight a sheer joy to read from start to finish.' *GracetheSpot.com*

The right of Shamim Sarif to be identified as the Author of the Work has been
asserted by her in accordance with the Copyright, Designs and Patents Act 1988.

The photographs used in this book have come from a variety of sources, including friends and
family, but for the official on and off-set shots I acknowledge the work of:

Blid Alsbirk *(The World Unseen)*
Claire Mason *(I Can't Think Straight)*
Adam Donneky *(I Can't Think Straight)*
Cathal Twomey *(Little Feeling and Broken)*
Anthony Harvey *(Little Feeling and Broken)*
Aida Kattan *(The World Unseen and various festivals)*
Cristina de la Madera *(Antwerp)*

Book designed by Laura Aloiso

10% of all sales of this book will go to Lisa Ray and her fight against cancer
via the Sarif-Kattan Foundation

First published in the United Kingdom by Enlightenment Press,
London, UK, 2010

ISBN 978-0-9560316-4-8

www.enlightenment-press.com